Level C

Vocabulary for Listening, Speaking, Reading, and Writing

Author

Jerry Zutell, Ph.D.

The Ohio State University

Credits: Located on last page of book

ISBN: 0-7367-2447-8

Copyright © 2005 Zaner-Bloser, Inc.

Zaner-Bloser, Inc., P.O. Box 16764, Columbus, Ohio 43216-6764 (1-800-421-3018)
www.zaner-bloser.com

A ZB Language Arts Program

Contents

4 UNIT THEME Living Things 72

5 UNIT THEME Work and Money 94

Contents **3**

**9 UNIT THEME
The Law**   **182**

Communication

PART 1

Context Clues

for Word Wisdom

Breaking the Silence:

Helen Keller

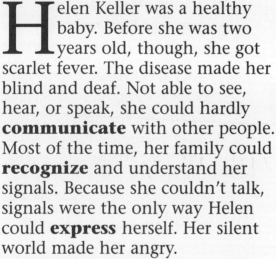

Have you heard of Helen Keller? She couldn't talk, hear, or see. Helen lived in a dark world without sound until one special person broke through the darkness and the silence.

Helen Keller was a healthy baby. Before she was two years old, though, she got scarlet fever. The disease made her blind and deaf. Not able to see, hear, or speak, she could hardly **communicate** with other people. Most of the time, her family could **recognize** and understand her signals. Because she couldn't talk, signals were the only way Helen could **express** herself. Her silent world made her angry.

When Helen was six years old, her parents hired a teacher named Annie Sullivan. Annie knew it would be hard to teach Helen. Helen usually did whatever she wanted. She would have to learn to give Annie her **attention**. Annie was firm with Helen. It was hard for Helen's parents to **admit** that Annie was right. After all, Helen didn't understand what was happening.

Annie used her fingers to spell words into Helen's hand. Helen thought Annie was playing a game. Then one day, everything changed. The **silence** of Helen's world was broken, and she suddenly understood.

Annie took Helen to the outdoor water pump. The cool water ran over Helen's hands. Annie spelled W-A-T-E-R into Helen's hands. Annie did this over and over. Finally, all of Annie's careful hard work, her **dedication,** made sense. For the first time, Helen understood that Annie's fingers were spelling out a word. Annie couldn't wait to make the exciting **announcement** that Helen now understood. When they heard the report, Helen's parents were **speechless**. They couldn't find words to express their thanks.

From that moment at the water pump, Helen understood that everything had a name. She was a quick learner. She soon had a new **vocabulary**. She had hundreds of words she could use. She was finally able to communicate. When Helen grew up, she became a teacher. She taught the world about communication.

Context Clues Strategy

Look for Words That Mean the Same

EXAMPLE: The red light *indicates,* or is a sign, that the cars will stop.

CLUE: In this sentence, the definition of *indicates* is already given. The words *is a sign* mean the same as the word *indicates.* The word *or* is a clue.

One way to understand new words is to use the context—the words that go with the new word. Here is one strategy.

Read the sentence with the unknown word.

*Finally, all of Annie's careful hard work, her **dedication,** made sense.*

Look for context clues. What **Words That Mean the Same** can you find?

The words *careful hard work* are a context clue for the word *dedication.* They mean the same as *dedication.*

Think about the context clues and what you already know about the word.

Dedication means "careful hard work" in the essay. I've heard people say that it takes dedication to do things, so that makes sense.

Predict a meaning for the word.

The word *dedication* must mean "careful hard work."

Check your Word Wisdom Dictionary to be sure of the meaning. Decide which of the meanings in the dictionary fits with the context.

Dedication means "service and time given to something important."

Practice the Strategy The word below is from the essay about Helen Keller on page 6. Use the context clues strategy on page 7 to figure out the meaning of the word.

announcement

📖 **Read** the sentence that uses the word *announcement*. Read some of the sentences around the word.

🔍 **Look** for context clues. What **Words That Mean the Same** can you find?

Report.

💡 **Think** about the context clues. What other helpful information do you know?

a exiting empotent report
New imformachan

➡️ **Predict** a meaning for the word *announcement*.

✔️ **Check** the Word Wisdom Dictionary to be sure of the meaning of the word *announcement*. Write the definition here.

WORD LIST

communicate

recognize

express

attention

admit

silence

✔ dedication

✔ announcement

speechless

vocabulary

Use Context Clues You have been introduced to two vocabulary words from the Helen Keller essay. Those words are checked off in the Word List here. Under "Vocabulary Word" below, write the other eight boldfaced words from the essay. Use your new context clues strategy to predict a possible meaning for each word under "Your Prediction." Then check the meanings in the Word Wisdom Dictionary. Write the definition under "Dictionary Says."

Vocabulary Word	Your Prediction	Dictionary Says
1 Communicate	a way to talk to each other	I communicate or shar idas with friend with emale
2 recognize	you Remember sombody or somthing	I Recognize that boy from his pictor
3 express	shoing your feelings	showing your feelings and thoughts
4 attention	Lisoning closly be attentiv	cosutating
5 admit	giving in	to agree sothing is tru
6 Silece	Very quiet	no sound
7 Speechles	your so suprised you cant speek	unable to speek
8 Vocabulary	a larg number of words	a word used by a group of people

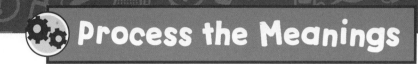

Process the Meanings

WORD LIST

communicate
recognize
express
attention
admit
silence
dedication
announcement
speechless
vocabulary

Find the Synonyms *Synonyms* are words that have the same or almost the same meaning. Match each synonym below with a word from the Word List. Write the word on the line.

Synonym	Vocabulary Word
1 words	vocabulary
2 quietness	silence
3 agree	admit
4 awareness	attention

Choose the Correct Word Write the word from the Word List that best completes each sentence.

5 Learning how to play a musical instrument takes patience and

dedication

6 I was so surprised that I didn't know what to say; I was

speechless

7 She looked so different that I did not recognize

_____ her.

8 If there is a blizzard, we'll listen to the radio for an

announcement about school closings.

9 When a person doesn't speak your language, it can be

difficult to communicate

10 I try to express myself clearly when I talk.

Apply What You've Learned

Relate the Meanings Answer each question.

1 Who usually makes the **announcements** in your school?

My teachers

2 When is it important to have **silence** in your classroom?

When we are getting instructions

3 What score on a test would leave you **speechless**? Why?

a 100

4 To whom do you have to pay **attention** in school?

To teachers

5 How can you show **dedication** to something?

Feed my goats every day

6 Why is it important to learn new **vocabulary**?

we could not read books

7 Why do some people find it hard to **admit** that they are wrong?

because they think thay are right

8 What is something you can easily **recognize** in your classroom?

The labels

9 What can you do to **express** yourself clearly?

Speek loudly

10 When does your teacher ask you to **communicate** in writing?

Fever most ofit time

Write It! Create a list of five things you can do to communicate clearly with your friends and family. Use Part 1 vocabulary words in your list.

PART 2 Latin Roots
for Word Wisdom

The Voice of Baseball:
Harry Caray

Have you ever listened to a baseball game on the radio? You get a different picture of the game if you listen, rather than watch, the game. People loved to listen to one man talk about baseball.

"Holy Cow!" Famous sports **announcer** Harry Caray said those words a lot. He used the saying when a team surprised him. He used the saying when a team excited him. Harry loved to **announce** baseball games.

In St. Louis, Missouri, a teenaged Harry got a job on the radio. He used his **vocal** talents to announce basketball and football games. But he wanted to work in baseball. After all, Harry was a baseball player himself.

Finally, Harry got his wish. He started announcing games for a baseball team, the St. Louis Cardinals. Harry stayed in this job for twenty-five years. But he did not stay there forever. He got a job in Chicago. There he announced baseball games for the Chicago White Sox and the Chicago Cubs.

Most baseball fans in Chicago remember Harry. He shared baseball games in a special way. Harry showed a lot of excitement. He said that he wanted to announce a game "the way a fan would." This included making mistakes. Harry often could not **pronounce,** or correctly say, some words. Harry knew he made some mistakes in **pronunciation**. He once said, "I've only been doing this for 54 years. With a little experience, I might get better." Harry made his listeners smile.

You had to hear Harry announce a game. You could not just read a **dictation,** or a written record, of what Harry said. You would not feel Harry's excitement. You would not hear Harry's unique **diction,** or his way of saying things. For example, Harry said "Holy Cow!" in a neat way. He stretched the **vowel** *o* in each word. It sounded like "Hoooly Cooow!"

Harry was not a **vocalist**, but he did sing during every game. He sang "Take Me Out to the Ball Game." Harry sang it during the seventh-inning stretch. This is a break in the middle of that inning. Fans sang the song with him.

Harry loved baseball. One reporter asked him to **predict** when he would retire. "Never," Harry replied. And he never did. Harry passed away in 1998. But he is remembered as the voice of baseball.

Practice the Context Clues Strategy Here is one of the boldfaced words from the essay on page 12. Use the context clues strategy you learned in Part 1 on page 7 to figure out the meaning of this word.

diction

📖 **Read** the sentence that uses the word *diction*. Read some of the sentences around the word.

🔍 **Look** for context clues to the word's meaning. What **Words That Mean the Same** can you find?

_____

_____

_____

💡 **Think** about the context clues. What other helpful information do you know?

_____

_____

_____

➡️ **Predict** a meaning for the word *diction*.

_____

_____

_____

✔️ **Check** your Word Wisdom Dictionary to be sure of the meaning of the word *diction*. Write the definition here.

_____

_____

_____

Many English words come from Latin roots. If you know the meanings of roots, you can often figure out the meanings of new words. Some of the words in Part 1 have a Latin root that is related to communication.

Latin Root: **dic, dict**	Latin Root: **nounce, nunci**	Latin Root: **voc**
meaning: to say	meaning: to announce	meaning: to call
English word: *dedication*	English word: *announcement*	English word: *vocabulary*
meaning: great loyalty	meaning: something said out loud publicly	meaning: words a person uses and understands

WORD LIST

announcer
announce
vocal
pronounce
pronunciation
dictation
diction
vowel
vocalist
predict

Sort by Roots Each word in the Word List comes from one of the three roots on this page. Write each word under its root. One word from *voc* has a different spelling. Then think of other words you know that come from the same Latin roots. Write those words, too.

Latin Root: dic, dict	Latin Root: nounce, nunci	Latin Root: voc
predict	announcer	vocalist
diction	announce	vocal
dictation	pronounce	invoke
dictionary	enunciate	vocalcord
adiction	pronunciation	vocation

Communication

Prefix	Meaning
pre-	before
pro-	forward, in favor of

Example

pre- (before) + **dict** (say) = **predict**

Use Roots and Prefixes Circle any root and prefix that you find in the boldfaced words. Use context clues, roots, and prefixes to write the meaning of each word. Check your definitions in the Word Wisdom Dictionary.

1 By looking at the dark clouds, we could **predict** that it would rain.

_____

2 The judge will **announce** the winner of the contest.

Something being said in publick

3 If you want to learn how to say this word, listen to its **pronunciation**.

the phonetic writing of a word

4 The letters *a, e, i, o,* and *u* are five **vowels** in the English alphabet.

Vowels are used alot in our languich

5 I gave an oral report, and my teacher said he liked my **diction**.

Speacking clearly

6 At the concert, the **vocalist** sang ten songs. a singer

7 At the ball game, the **announcer** gave the score.

Some one who brings somethin to publick attention

8 During **dictation** exercises, my teacher reads a sentence aloud.

matereal writen down for someone who said it

9 You could hear Bill's good **vocal** ability as he gave his speech.

made or performed from voice

10 You can **pronounce** the word *read* in two different ways.

How you say something

WORD LIST

- announcer
- announce
- vocal
- pronounce
- pronunciation
- dictation
- diction
- vowel
- vocalist
- predict

Match the Meaning Write the best word from the Word List to take the place of the underlined words in each sentence. You may need to add an ending to some words.

1 The words *library* and *spaghetti* can be hard words to <u>say correctly</u>.

pronounce

2 I can <u>say in advance</u> that our team will win the game.

predict

3 The word *automobile* has all the <u>letters *a, e, i, o,* and *u*</u>.

vowels

4 Speech class has helped me with my <u>way of saying words</u>.

pronunciation

5 Tim's <u>singing</u> performance was great!

vocal

6 The <u>person who reads the news on the radio</u> has a cold.

announcer

7 My sister wishes that she could be a famous <u>singer</u>.

vocalist

8 At the end of recess, my teacher always <u>states loudly</u> that it's time to go back to class.

anounces

9 We learn new vocabulary to improve our <u>choice of words</u>.

diction

10 We listen to our teacher and <u>write down spelling words</u>.

dictate

Apply What You've Learned

Use Words to Explain Follow the directions.

1 Explain why two people who are arguing are being **vocal**.

they are making sound and sound comes from your vocal chords

2 Tell what an **announcer** does during a baseball game.

he is reporting to people about wats going on in the game

3 Why is it good to **predict** the weather before going on a trip?

because you migh pack the wrong things

4 Tell about a famous **vocalist** you know.

one of my best friends dad is reciccl man

5 Explain why a teacher needs to have good **diction**.

for her or his students to understand wat their saying

Demonstrate Word Knowledge Answer the questions.

6 What types of words are difficult for you to **pronounce**?

Spanish words

7 How many **vowels** are in the English alphabet?

5 but if you count y it is 6

8 Why does a secretary need to be skilled at taking **dictation**?

if they are not skilled they might write something important wrong

9 What is the difference between **announce** and **pronounce**?

announce means to talk in publick and pronounce is how talk

10 What teacher helps students with their **pronunciation**?

Speach therapests

Speak It! Ask if you can give the school announcements tomorrow. Be the announcer for the day!

PART 3 Reference Skills

for Word Wisdom

Debates:

Communicating With Voters

Every four years, the people of the United States choose a president. How do they pick a person to vote for? How do they know who will make the best president? First, voters learn about the candidates—then they make their choice.

A candidate is a person who is up for election. A candidate wants people to know what he or she believes in. Candidates are written about in newspapers. They appear on television specials. People listen to what the candidates have to say. They **discuss** the candidates' ideas with their friends. Talking with others helps people form their own opinions about the candidates and about the issues.

Debates help people make choices about how to vote. People **debate,** or talk about, certain topics. Candidates running for president of the United States often have debates. Many people watch the debates on TV.

In a debate, the candidates **state** their ideas. They talk about important subjects and they answer many questions. One person might **reply** to what another person said. Someone might **complain** about another's ideas.

Most debates have a moderator. A moderator is like a referee. This person makes sure the debate goes smoothly. If a candidate does not answer a question properly, the moderator can **demand** a better answer. If a candidate talks for too long, the moderator can **urge** him or her to finish. The moderator also **narrates** the debate's events for the audience.

Sometimes, a group of experts are chosen to take part in a debate. They ask the candidates questions. Newspaper reporters are often a part of presidential debates. Reporters are good at asking the right questions. Every day, they **report** on important events in the world.

Another kind of debate is called a "town hall" debate. This is when anyone can be a part of the action. Anyone can **request** a topic for the candidates to talk about.

Many things help voters make their choice. But one thing is for sure: People have to learn as much as possible about the candidates. That is the only way to decide which candidate is right for you.

Practice the Context Clues Strategy Here is one of the boldfaced words from the essay on page 18. Use the context clues strategy you learned in Part 1 on page 7 to figure out the meaning of this word.

discuss

Read the sentence that uses the word *discuss*. Read some of the sentences around the word.

Look for context clues to the word's meaning. What **Words That Mean the Same** can you find?

talking with others

Think about the context clues. What other helpful information do you know?

talking with more than one person

Predict a meaning for the word *discuss*.

talk with a nother person(s) about something

Check your Word Wisdom Dictionary to be sure of the meaning of the word *discuss*. Write the definition here.

to talk about

Alphabetical Order Words in a dictionary are arranged in alphabetical order. You can find a word in a dictionary by looking at the first letter of the word.

When words begin with the same letter, look at the second, third, or fourth letter to put the words in alphabetical order. For example, the three words below from the Word List on page 21 all begin with the letter *r*. The second letter of each word is *e*. So, look at the third letter. The letter *p* comes before *q* in the alphabet, so *reply* and *report* come before *request*. Then, *reply* would come before *report* once you put the fourth letters—*l* and *o*—in alphabetical order.

1. reply
2. report
3. request

Use Alphabetical Order Put the words from the Word List on page 21 in alphabetical order. Look at the first, second, third, or even fourth letters to decide on the correct order. Check your final order in the Word Wisdom Dictionary.

1. complain
2. debate
3. demand
4. discuss
5. narrate

6. reply
7. report
8. request
9. state
10. urge

Find the Meaning

1. Use context clues.
2. Look for a familiar root, prefix, or suffix.
3. If the context or a word part doesn't help, check the dictionary.

Define the Words Follow the three steps above to write the meaning of each boldfaced word. Then write 1, 2, or 3 to show which steps you used. Check your answers in a dictionary.

WORD LIST

discuss
debate
state
reply
complain
demand
urge
narrate
report
request

1 After you get my letter, please **reply** by writing back to me.

_2._

2 Kevin raced to the phone to **report** the fire.

_2._

3 If you don't want to talk now, we can **discuss** things later.

_3._

4 I looked at the book while my teacher **narrated** the story.

_3._

5 My friend **requested** that we wear a costume to her party.

_2._

6 If I bother my little brother, he **complains** to my mother.

_3._

7 My friend **urged** me to go on the roller coaster with him.

_3._

8 On the first day, we **stated** our names clearly.

_3._

9 We **debated** whether to go to the movies or to go ice-skating.

_3._

10 I **demand** to know who read my diary.

_3._

WORD LIST

- discuss
- debate
- state
- reply
- complain
- demand
- urge
- narrate
- report
- request

Choose the Correct Word Write the best word from the Word List to complete each sentence. You may need to add an ending to some words.

1 My neighbor will _complain_ if anyone throws trash on her lawn.

2 The manager politely _requested_ that theater guests be quiet during the movie.

3 We will all meet today to _discuss_ ideas for the class trip.

4 When you want something, ask politely. Do not _demand_ things.

5 There's really no need for us to argue. Let's not _debate_ this topic any longer.

6 Please speak loudly and _state_ your question clearly.

7 If you witness a crime, you should _report_ it to the police.

8 Every day after lunch, we listen to my teacher _narrate_ a short story.

9 When I'm bored, my mother _urges_ me to read a good book.

10 I sent a letter to my cousin. Now I am waiting for him to _reply_.

Demonstrate Word Knowledge Choose the best word from the Word List for each situation. Use the word in a sentence to answer the question.

1 Sam hates shopping. What does he do when he has to shop?

complain

2 How can Amy and Jen get permission to do a project together?

request

3 Mr. Brodsky retells old stories. How does he tell them?

narrates

4 Mike hates vegetables. How does Dad get Mike to eat salad?

urges

5 If you see anything strange, tell the police. What do you do?

report

6 Mrs. Silver wants a refund. How will she insist on a refund?

demand

7 How do Mom and her friends talk about world events?

discussing

8 How did Lin say her name and address for her driver's license?

stated

9 How would two people prove they are right?

debate

10 I asked John a question. Now what do I want him to do?

reply

Write It! Write a letter to a friend urging him or her to do something good. Use as many words from Part 3 as you can.

Review

for Word Wisdom

Sort by First Letter Look at each word in the Word List. What letter does the word begin with? Write it in the correct column of the chart. Look for the roots *dic, dict* (to say), *nounce, nunci* (to announce), and *voc* (to call). If a word has one of those roots, circle the word. Remember that one word from *voc* has a different spelling.

WORD LIST

- communicate
- recognize
- express
- attention
- admit
- silence
- dedication
- announcement
- speechless
- vocabulary
- announcer
- announce
- vocal
- pronounce
- pronunciation
- dictation
- diction
- vowel
- vocalist
- predict
- discuss
- debate
- state
- reply
- complain
- demand
- urge
- narrate
- report
- request

a–d	e–r	s–z
attention	express	silence
admit	prounce	speechless
announcement	pronunciation	state
announcer	predict	urge
announce	recognize	vocabulary
communicate	reply	vocal
dedication	report	vowel
dictation	request	vocalist
diction	narrate	
discuss		
debate		
demand		
complain		

Replace the Boldfaced Words Choose a word from the Word List that could replace the boldfaced word or words.

1 Give **notice** to the lifeguard when you are swimming.

attention

2 Did you learn any new **words** today?

vocabulary

3 Everyone clapped after the **singer** performed.

vocalist

4 The **radio message** stated that school was closed because of the snowstorm. _announcer_

5 Learning how to play the violin takes a lot of **hard work and practice.** _dedication_

Identify Antonyms Choose a word from the Word List to complete each phrase.

6 not a **consonant**, but a _vowel_

7 not to **ask** a question, but to _reply_ with an answer

8 not **noise**, but _silence_

9 not a **quiet** person, but a _vocal_ person

10 not **full of things to say**, but _speechless_

Taking Vocabulary Tests

Practice Test   Read each sentence. Fill in the circle for the word that best completes each sentence.

1 I _____ that you were right.

○ complain

◉ admit

○ narrate

2 During the play, there was _____ in the audience.

○ diction

○ reply

◉ silence

3 I will _____ one thing of you.

◉ request

○ report

○ express

4 Can you _____ what will happen next?

○ reply

○ urge

◉ predict

5 That unhappy boy always _____.

○ narrates

◉ complains

○ announces

6 Brendan talks a lot. He is loud and _____.

○ vocalist

◉ vocal

○ vowel

7 Did you hear today's _____ over the loudspeaker?

○ vocabulary

◉ announcement

○ dictation

8 Can you _____ this long word?

◉ pronounce

○ request

○ demand

9 My parents _____ me to work hard in school.

○ debate

○ reply

◉ urge

10 His hard work shows so much _____.

◉ dedication

○ diction

○ pronunciation

Build New Words

Use Suffixes A suffix is a word ending. The suffix *-er* or *-or* means "a person who." If you add *-er* or *-or* to a verb, you will make a noun that names a kind of person:

verb		suffix		noun
run	+	-er	=	runner

Add the suffix *-er* or *-or* to make a new word. Check the Word Wisdom Dictionary if you don't know whether the new word should end in *-er* or *-or*. Then write a sentence using each new word.

Word	+ Suffix	= New Word	Sentence
report	er	reporter	I saw a reporter at the enoguration for presadent Obama
narrate	or	narator	the narrator reading the book on tape sounded funny
announce	er	announcer	The announcer said ther would be rain today
predict	or	predictor	Nancy drew is a great predictor of school lunches
complain	er	complainer	youre a complainer said the girl

Speak It! Pretend you can have one wish come true. What would you wish for? How would your life change? Tell about your wish and what would happen if you got it. Use as many words as you can from this Communication unit.

Context Clues

for Word Wisdom

Guide Dogs:
The Eyes of Their Owners

Guide dogs are special dogs with a special job. Perhaps you've seen a guide dog with its owner at a park or in a restaurant. Read this essay to find out more about guide dogs.

Guide dogs are also known as Seeing Eye dogs. These **spectacular** animals are not ordinary dogs. They are dogs that help blind people. A guide dog and its owner have a special team relationship.

A guide dog and its owner work together to move from one place to another. The owner directs the dog with commands such as "right," "left," and "forward." The dogs also learn their owner's usual routes. The owner can say, "Go to the mailbox" or "Find the door." The dog will lead its owner to the place.

Guide dogs have amazing memories. After the owner and dog **visit** a new place just once or twice, the dog may remember how to get there again. Unlike pet dogs, guide dogs can go with their owners to restaurants and stores and on airplanes and buses.

Guide dogs help their owners cross busy streets. A guide dog stops at a street curb. The owner can **sense** when it is safe to cross. The owner listens to the flow of traffic. Guide dogs can't read **signals** such as traffic lights because they are colorblind. If a situation is unsafe or if a dog is confused, it won't lead its owner into danger. Only when it is **evident** that there is no danger will the dog continue.

When the guide dog is working, it must be **alert,** not sleepy or un-watchful. The guide dog is trained to deal with **unforeseen** things. It leads its owner around people, cars, and bicycles. If the owner and dog suddenly come to a flight of stairs, the dog will stop. This tells the owner that he or she must use caution before going farther.

Guide dogs **fascinate** most people. If you **glance** at a guide dog with its owner, you should respect the team. You should not **distract** the dog. Do not call, pet, or feed the dog. The dog needs to concentrate and pay attention. Guide dogs have a serious job.

Guide dogs normally work for eight to ten years. During that time, they become the "eyes" of their owner.

Context Clues Strategy

Look for Words That Mean the Opposite

EXAMPLE: We couldn't see the bottom of the pond because the water was *murky*, not clear.

CLUE: The word *clear* means the opposite of *murky*. An opposite tells differences in meanings.

One way to understand the meaning of a new word is to use the context—the words that go with the new word. Here is another strategy for using context clues to understand new words.

Read the sentence with the unknown word.

*When the guide dog is working, it must be **alert**, not sleepy or unwatchful.*

Look for context clues. What **Words That Mean the Opposite** of **alert** can you find?

The words *sleepy* and *unwatchful* mean the opposite of the word **alert**.

Think about the context clues and other information you already know.

People who are about to fall asleep are not alert.

Predict a meaning for the word.

The word **alert** must mean "awake and watchful."

Check the Word Wisdom Dictionary to be sure of the meaning. Decide which of the meanings in the dictionary fits the context.

In this context, **alert** means "watchful."

Unlock the Meanings

Practice the Strategy The word below is from the "Guide Dogs" essay on page 28. Use the context clues strategy on page 29 to figure out the meaning of the word.

spectacular

Read the sentence that uses the word *spectacular*. Read some of the sentences around the word.

Look for context clues to the word's meaning. What **Words That Mean the Opposite** can you find?

_____

_____

_____

Think about the context clues. What other helpful information do you know?

_____

_____

_____

Predict a meaning for the word *spectacular*.

_____

_____

_____

Check your Word Wisdom Dictionary to be sure of the meaning of the word *spectacular*. Write the definition here.

_____

_____

_____

WORD LIST

✔ spectacular
  visit
  sense
  signal
  evident
✔ alert
  unforeseen
  fascinate
  glance
  distract

Use Context Clues   You have been introduced to two vocabulary words from "Guide Dogs: The Eyes of Their Owners." Those words are checked off in the Word List here. Under "Vocabulary Word" below, write the other eight words from the Word List. Use context clues to write a possible meaning for each word under "Your Prediction." Then check the meanings in the Word Wisdom Dictionary. Write the definition under "Dictionary Says."

	Vocabulary Word	Your Prediction	Dictionary Says
1			
2			
3			
4			
5			
6			
7			
8			

WORD LIST

spectacular

visit

sense

signal

evident

alert

unforeseen

fascinate

glance

distract

Use the Words Correctly in Writing Rewrite each sentence in your own words. Include the word in parentheses. You may need to change the ending of the word.

1 When you hear the whistle, you should run. (signal)

_____

2 Can we spend some time at the park today? (visit)

_____

3 Don't make noise while Dad is working. (distract)

_____

4 There was a wonderful fireworks display. (spectacular)

_____

5 I can tell that you don't believe me. (evident)

_____

6 I couldn't take my eyes off the dolphin show. (fascinate)

_____

7 I could feel that Jake was angry with me. (sense)

_____

8 When I get enough sleep, I pay better attention. (alert)

_____

9 Jill looked at the newspaper quickly before work. (glance)

_____

10 Our train was delayed when it broke down. (unforeseen)

_____

Apply What You've Learned

Complete the Sentences Finish each sentence.

1 Magic shows **fascinate** people because

_____

2 I have to be **alert** during a spelling test because

_____

3 The tightrope act in the circus is **spectacular** because

_____

4 Runners need a **signal** to begin a race because

_____

5 Sometimes my dad **glances** at his watch because

_____

6 It is important to **visit** the dentist because

_____

7 It was **evident** that it had rained because

_____

8 My mother could **sense** that I was unhappy because

_____

9 Don't **distract** a person driving a car because

_____

10 The change in weather was **unforeseen** because

_____

 Write It! Write about something in nature that fascinates you. Use several words from the Word List on page 32.

PART 2

Latin Roots

for Word Wisdom

The Audience as Actors:

Participation Theater

Sometimes, you sit and watch a play. Other times, you act in a play. But did you know that you could do both at once?

Have you ever been in a play? Have you ever watched a play? Imagine if you could do both at the same time! You buy a ticket. You go to the play as a **spectator**. Then, in a flash, you are an actor in the play!

There are many kinds of plays that include the audience. In Playback Theater, an audience member tells about a **significant** day in his or her life. Then the actors make a short play out of the story. The audience member's story is **visible** right before his or her eyes! The actors do not **revise,** or change, the story. They simply act it out for the audience to enjoy.

Another kind of play is called Involvement Theater. Audience members work with actors during the play. This kind of theater is often used to teach certain skills to children. The play might show how to solve problems. It might show how to get along with others or how to handle one's feelings. These plays can be **especially** helpful for students in grade school and middle school.

Participation Theater is another fun kind of play. In one popular play, audience members are guests at a wedding. You **view** the marriage service. You put your **signature** in the guest book. You eat dinner. You can even dance the night away!

A really fun kind of play is called Mystery Dinner Theater. While the audience eats dinner, actors show a mystery. Then the dinner guests try to solve the mystery. They think about the events. They focus on things that **signify** something important. They decide which characters are **suspicious** and which characters can be trusted. Then they tell who they think committed the crime. In some plays, even audience members can be **suspected** of the crime!

So the next time you want to see a play, try one that you can be a part of. You might have a lot of fun. You might even decide to become an actor yourself!

Practice the Context Clues Strategy   Here is one of the boldfaced words from the essay on page 34. Use the context clues strategy you learned in Part 1 on page 29 to figure out the meaning of this word.

suspicious

Read the sentence that uses the word *suspicious*. Read some of the sentences around the word.

Look for context clues to the word's meaning. Are there **Words That Mean the Opposite** of *suspicious*?

_____

_____

_____

Think about the context clues. What other helpful information do you know?

_____

_____

_____

Predict a meaning for the word *suspicious*.

_____

_____

_____

Check your Word Wisdom Dictionary to be sure of the meaning of the word *suspicious*. Which of the meanings for the word *suspicious* fits the context?

_____

_____

_____

Unlock the Meanings

Many English words are made from Latin roots. If you know the meaning of different roots, you can unlock the meaning of many new words. Several words you learned in Part 1 have Latin roots. Each root is related to ways of seeing.

Latin Root: **spec, spect, spic**
meaning: to look, to see
English word: *spectacular*
meaning: sensational

Latin Root: **sign**
meaning: sign, mark
English word: *signal*
meaning: something that gives a message

Latin Root: **vid, vis**
meaning: to see
English word: *visit*
meaning: to spend time in a place

WORD LIST

- spectator
- significant
- visible
- revise
- especially
- view
- signature
- signify
- suspicious
- suspect

Sort by Roots Find these roots in the Word List. Write each word in the correct group.

Sight

Latin Root: spec, spect, spic	Latin Root: sign	Latin Root: vid, vis

Prefix	Meaning
re-	again, back

Example

re- (again) + vise (see) = revise

Use Roots and Prefixes Circle any roots or prefixes that you find in the boldfaced words below. Use roots, prefixes, and context clues to write the meaning of each word. Check your definitions in a dictionary.

1 My birthday is a **significant** day in my life every year.

_____

2 The balloons on the front door **signify** that the party is here.

_____

3 I wasn't part of the race. I was only a **spectator**.

_____

4 After I do my homework, my mother writes her **signature** on it.

_____

5 When you didn't answer the door, I **suspected** you weren't home.

_____

6 Look through this telescope to **view** the stars.

_____

7 Our plan isn't working. We need to **revise** it and try again.

_____

8 Grace's eyes aren't **visible** under her big hat.

_____

9 The dog with the cake on its face strikes me as **suspicious**.

_____

10 Mrs. Fisher helps everyone. She is an **especially** kind person.

_____

Process the Meanings

WORD LIST

- spectator
- significant
- visible
- revise
- especially
- view
- signature
- signify
- suspicious
- suspect

Choose the Correct Word Write the word from the Word List that best completes each sentence. You will need to add an **-s** to two words.

1 Make sure your teacher's _____ is on the permission slip.

2 If you stand on the hilltop, you can

_____ the city in the distance.

3 I will _____ my paragraph to fix the

mistakes and make it better.

4 Nina is a wonderful artist. She is _____ talented at drawing people.

5 I have chills and a high fever. My mother

_____ that I have the flu.

6 A germ is tiny. It is not _____ to the human eye.

7 I don't understand what these marks mean. What do they

_____?

8 The restaurant closed earlier than usual, and all the lights

are out. Something looks _____.

9 Graduation is a special and _____ event.

10 When the player hit a home run, the

_____ clapped and cheered.

Apply What You've Learned

Demonstrate Word Knowledge Answer the questions below.

1 What does a **spectator** do at the circus?

_____

2 What foods are **especially** sweet?

_____

3 What can you **view** from a window in your home?

_____

4 What could a frown on a person's face **signify**?

_____

5 When you write a letter, where do you put your **signature**?

_____

6 What would you do to **revise** a report?

_____

7 What is something that is **visible** only at night?

_____

8 What would you **suspect** if your friend wasn't at school?

_____

9 Who is a **significant** person in your life? Why?

_____

10 Why might you be **suspicious** if a dog suddenly barked?

_____

Speak It! Describe a funny object that your friends would have to see to believe. Use as many words as you can from the Word List on page 38.

PART 3 Reference Skills

A View Into the Past:

The La Brea Tar Pits

You can often find important things in unlikely places. This happened in downtown Los Angeles. An area called the La Brea Tar Pits holds secrets to the past.

When you think of Los Angeles, do you see a city with beaches and movie stars? You probably don't think of science. But there is a place in L.A. where science takes you 40,000 years into the past!

A hundred years ago, the La Brea Tar Pit area was a **mysterious** place. But through the years, scientists have learned much about the area. For **example,** they have learned that the tar pits formed about 40,000 years ago during the last Ice Age. They also know that the substance in the pits is not tar—it is asphalt. This sticky substance bubbles up through the ground and collects in pools.

Long ago, leaves covered these pools. This made the sticky asphalt hard to see. A passing animal would step into the pool and get stuck. It could not move. It was only a matter of time before the substance would **extinguish** the animal's life.

Other animals, like wolves, would see a trapped animal. The wolves might have thought it was a **mirage**—why would a huge bison stand still when wolves came near? But it was real. The bison was stuck. The wolves would go in for an easy dinner, but they would get stuck as well.

Animal after animal became trapped in the pits. **Traces** of these animals remained. La Brea became a kind of photo **album** of the past. Animal bones pressed against rocks to form fossils. These fossils are like snapshots—scientists can determine what these animals looked like, when they lived, and what they ate. These pictures of the past help scientists understand the **scope** of certain time periods. They can then understand the past of the Los Angeles area.

Scientists learned about many **extinct** animals, like saber-toothed cats and dire wolves. They also learned about plants and animals that are still alive today. Many of the La Brea fossils are on **display** in the George C. Page Museum. Visitors can see the tar pits as a **symbol** of a different Los Angeles.

Practice the Context Clues Strategy Here is one of the boldfaced words from the essay on page 40. Use the context clues strategy you learned in Part 1 on page 29 to figure out the meaning of this word.

extinct

Read the sentence that uses the word *extinct*. Read some of the sentences around the word.

Look for context clues to the word's meaning. Are there **Words That Mean the Opposite** of *extinct*?

_____

_____

_____

Think about the context clues. What other helpful information do you know?

_____

_____

_____

Predict a meaning for the word *extinct*.

_____

_____

_____

Check your Word Wisdom Dictionary to be sure of the meaning of the word *extinct*. Write the definition here.

_____

_____

_____

Unlock the Meanings

Alphabetical Order A dictionary is arranged in alphabetical order. You will find every word under its first letter. All words that start with the same letter are alphabetized by the second letter. When the first two letters are the same, the words are alphabetized by the third letter, and so on.

Alphabetize to the Second Letter Write each group of words in alphabetical order.

1 symbol, see, survey _____ _____ _____

2 gaze, guard, goggles _____ _____ _____

3 look, lurk, light _____ _____ _____

4 present, picture, peek _____ _____ _____

5 observe, optic, ocular _____ _____ _____

Alphabetize to the Third Letter Number each word to show which would come first in the dictionary **1** and which would come second **2**. Write the letters that you used to decide.

6 scope _____ Three letters of word 1: _____

   scene _____ Three letters of word 2: _____

7 example _____ Three letters of word 1: _____

   extinct _____ Three letters of word 2: _____

8 glance _____ Three letters of word 1: _____

   glimpse _____ Three letters of word 2: _____

9 vision _____ Three letters of word 1: _____

   view _____ Three letters of word 2: _____

10 mirage _____ Three letters of word 1: _____

   migrate _____ Three letters of word 2: _____

Find the Meaning

1. Use context clues.
2. Look for a familiar root, prefix, or suffix.
3. If the context or a word part doesn't help, check the dictionary.

Define the Words   Follow the steps above to write the meaning of each boldfaced word. Write 1, 2, or 3 to show which steps you used.

WORD LIST

| mysterious |
| example |
| extinguish |
| mirage |
| trace |
| album |
| scope |
| extinct |
| display |
| symbol |

1 My dog disappeared without a **trace**.

_____

2 Our teacher will **display** our projects on a table in the hallway.

_____

3 Dinosaurs are **extinct** creatures.

_____

4 The dove is a **symbol** of peace.

_____

5 Let's look at the photos in the **album**.

_____

6 After we **extinguished** the candles, the room was dark.

_____

7 A snake is an **example** of an animal that sheds its skin.

_____

8 We can't figure out why the lights went out. It's **mysterious**.

_____

9 The thirsty man thought he saw water, but it was a **mirage**.

_____

10 I wish I understood the **scope** of building a tree house.

_____

Process the Meanings

WORD LIST

- mysterious
- example
- extinguish
- mirage
- trace
- album
- scope
- extinct
- display
- symbol

Choose the Correct Word Write the word from the Word List that best completes each sentence. Underline the parts of the sentence that helped you make your decision. The first one is done for you.

1 I keep my sticker collection in an _____ album _____.

2 Because of water pollution, scientists fear that some fish will become _____.

3 I thought I saw a castle. It turned out to be only a _____.

4 You cleaned very well. There is not a _____ of dust on the furniture.

5 I don't understand how to do this math problem. Could you write another _____ on the board?

6 I _____ my favorite seashells on a shelf for everyone to see.

7 Before we leave the campsite, we must _____ the campfire.

8 Our faucet leaked. Before he came, the plumber wanted to know the _____ of the problem.

9 Who is that unusual and _____ woman who just walked past our classroom?

10 A red heart is a _____ of love.

Apply What You've Learned

1 Name one **symbol** and tell what it means.

_____

2 Name two **examples** of mammals.

_____

3 Name two things people often keep in an **album**.

_____

4 Name three things that are in your **scope** of ability.

_____

5 Name two things that you would like to **display** in your room.

_____

Solve the Riddle Write a word from the Word List on page 44 for each clue.

_____ **6** I'm not really there. I'm in your imagination.

_____ **7** I could be fingerprints left behind at a crime scene.

_____ **8** You just can't figure me out.

_____ **9** I was alive in the past, but I'm no longer around.

_____ **10** You'll sleep better if you do this to the lights.

Write It! Write a riddle for three more words from the Word List on page 44. Don't choose the same words that solve the riddles above. Begin each riddle with the word *I* or *You.*

PART 4

WORD LIST

- spectacular
- visit
- sense
- signal
- evident
- alert
- unforeseen
- fascinate
- glance
- distract
- spectator
- significant
- visible
- revise
- especially
- view
- signature
- signify
- suspicious
- suspect
- mysterious
- example
- extinguish
- mirage
- trace
- album
- scope
- extinct
- display
- symbol

Review for Word Wisdom

Sort by Final Letters Look at each word in the Word List. What letter does the word end with? Write the word in the correct column of the chart.

Now study each word. Look for the roots *spec, spect, spic* (to look, to see), *sign* (a sign, a mark), and *vid, vis* (to see). If a word has one of those roots, circle the root.

Words ending in e	Words ending in t	Words ending in other letters

Check the Meanings Read each phrase. Do the words go together? If they do, write **yes**. If they don't, write **no**. If you write **no,** write a new word to go with the boldfaced word.

1 **extinct** dinosaur _____

2 **extinguish** a lake _____

3 **revise** a report _____

4 telephone **album** _____

5 **suspicious** pencil _____

Demonstrate Word Knowledge Answer the questions.

6 Can you **view** something that is **visible**? Why or why not?

_____

7 What's an **example** of something **especially** tasty?

_____

8 Why can't you **visit** a **mirage**?

_____

9 Is it all right for a **spectator** to **distract** a ballplayer? Why or why not?

_____

_____

10 If you had a pencil on your desk, and now there is no **trace** of it, what would you **suspect** had happened?

_____

_____

Taking Vocabulary Tests

Sample:

suspicious

○ surprising
○ unusual
● distrustful
○ beautiful

Practice Test Fill in the circle of the word that has the SAME or ALMOST THE SAME meaning as the boldfaced word. If you can't decide on an answer, go on. Come back to the item after you've answered the other items.

1 mysterious
○ simple
○ strange
○ clear
○ difficult

2 display
○ ignore
○ show
○ watch
○ go

3 spectator
○ judge
○ stadium
○ observer
○ announcer

4 unforeseen
○ unexpected
○ understood
○ inside
○ enough

5 significant
○ different
○ light
○ tiny
○ important

6 symbol
○ exercise
○ sign
○ tool
○ event

7 evident
○ obvious
○ careful
○ great
○ silly

8 signify
○ hide
○ hear
○ mean
○ read

9 fascinate
○ prevent
○ continue
○ scream
○ amaze

10 alert
○ asleep
○ aware
○ angry
○ alone

Solve the Mystery Message For each clue, write a word from the Word List on page 46. When you are finished, find a mystery message! Copy the letters above the numbered spaces onto the matching numbered lines at the bottom of the page. You'll find out what a guard must do.

1 the range of your ideas or abilities: __ __ __ __ __
                                           1

2 your handwritten name: __ __ __ __ __ __ __ __
                              3   9

3 feel: __ __ __ __ __
           7

4 strange: __ __ __ __ __ __ __ __ __ __
               2   8

5 show: __ __ __ __ __ __ __
            6   5   4

A guard must __ __ __ __   __ __ __ __ __!
             1 2 3 4   5 6 7 8 9

Speak It! Tell your class a good mystery story. If you need some ideas, here are some story starters: a mysterious spectator at your soccer game, something significant that disappears without a trace, or a suspicious signature on a letter you receive. Use several of the words from the Word List on page 46.

PART 1

Context Clues

for Word Wisdom

The Monarch Butterfly:

Butterflies on the Move

Monarch butterflies are those beautiful butterflies with the black and orange wings. During the spring and summer, you may spot one fluttering around your yard or a park. When it gets colder, what happens to them? Read this article to find out.

In the fall, monarch butterflies fly south. Like birds, they must go south to survive the winter. Their journey begins up north in the United States or Canada. It ends in a small area of Mexico. The butterflies return to this same place year after year.

Monarch butterflies amaze scientists. It isn't clear how the butterflies know their way to Mexico. They seem to have a built-in **compass** that points them in the right direction. Using the sun as a guide, they travel south. It takes the butterflies a few months to make their journey. The trip is thousands of miles long.

Along their **route,** the butterflies sip nectar from flowers. This gives them energy. The monarchs fly during the early part of the day. If you spot them during their trip south, you may see a few, or even hundreds, flying **across** the sky.

In a single day, the monarch butterfly can fly quite far. Scientists know this from an experiment. They **captured** some butterflies and put tags on them. Then the scientists **released** the butterflies so that they could continue on their journey. The following day, one of the tagged butterflies was recaptured. It had flown more than 250 miles!

The butterflies are able to travel so far because they **glide** with the wind. They fly smoothly and easily. They don't travel far by flapping their wings. That takes too much energy. Like birds that fly high in the air, monarch butterflies use air currents to rise in the air and **soar**. With their wings spread wide, they ride on the wind.

Each butterfly goes on its journey alone. At night, however, the butterflies **cluster**. They gather in bunches and crowd together on tree branches. Hundreds can be seen, quiet and **stationary,** covering the trees. Although the butterflies don't have eyelids to shut their eyes, they do rest. In the morning, they **ascend** into the air once again and go on their way.

Context Clues Strategy

Look for What Kind of Thing the Word Is

EXAMPLE: Moving their wings quickly and lightly, the butterflies *fluttered* in the air.

CLUE: The phrase *moving their wings quickly and lightly* tells what kind of action *fluttered* is.

Here is another strategy for using context clues to understand new words.

Read the sentence with the unknown word. Read a sentence or two around it.

*The butterflies are able to travel so far because they **glide** with the wind. They fly smoothly and easily.*

Look for context clues. Which words tell you **What Kind of Thing the Word Is?**

The words *fly smoothly and easily* tell what kind of action *glide* is.

Think about the context clues and other information you already know.

I know that paper airplanes glide through the air.

Predict a meaning for the word.

The word *glide* must mean "to fly smoothly and easily."

Check the Word Wisdom Dictionary to be sure of the meaning.

The word *glide* means "to move smoothly."

Practice the Strategy Here is another boldfaced word from the article about monarch butterflies on page 50. Use the context clues strategy on page 51 to figure out the meaning of the word.

---- cluster ----

📖 **Read** the sentence that uses the word *cluster*. Read some of the sentences around the word.

🔍 **Look** for context clues to the word's meaning. What words can you find that tell **What Kind of Thing** *cluster* is?

_____

_____

_____

💡 **Think** about the context clues. What other helpful information do you know?

_____

_____

_____

➡️ **Predict** a meaning for the word *cluster*.

_____

_____

_____

✔️ **Check** your Word Wisdom Dictionary to be sure of the meaning of the word *cluster*. Which meaning for the word *cluster* fits the context?

_____

_____

_____

Use Context Clues The two vocabulary words that you have learned so far are checked off in the Word List. In the first column, write the other eight words from the Word List. Use context clues to predict a meaning for each word in the second column. Then check the meanings in the Word Wisdom Dictionary. In the third column, write the definition that fits the context.

WORD LIST

compass

route

across

capture

release

✔ glide

soar

✔ cluster

stationary

ascend

Vocabulary Word	Your Prediction	Dictionary Says
1		
2		
3		
4		
5		
6		
7		
8		

Process the Meanings

WORD LIST

- compass
- route
- across
- capture
- release
- glide
- soar
- cluster
- stationary
- ascend

Find the Opposite Choose a word from the Word List that is the OPPOSITE or NEARLY THE OPPOSITE of the word or words. Write your answer on the line.

1 moving _____

2 to hold _____

3 to free _____

4 to spread out _____

5 not a specific path _____

Choose the Correct Word Read each sentence. Write the word from the Word List that best completes each sentence. Use each word only once.

6 I hit the tennis ball _____ the court.

7 By climbing the stairs, we _____ to the next floor.

8 During our hike, we used a _____ to point us in the right direction.

9 Watch these toy boats. They _____ so smoothly down the stream.

10 Looking up, we love to see the airplanes

_____ high in the sky.

Apply What You've Learned

Demonstrate Word Knowledge   Answer the questions below.

1 Why might you need to use a **compass**?

_____

2 Why might you want to ride on a **stationary** bicycle?

_____

3 How might you travel **across** a river?

_____

4 Why might you want to **capture** a bug?

_____

5 Why might you be **released** from school early?

_____

6 When might you **glide** on ice?

_____

7 How might you **ascend** to the fourth floor of a building?

_____

8 Why might you need to find a new **route** to a friend's house?

_____

9 When might your hopes **soar**?

_____

10 Why might students **cluster** around their teacher?

_____

Write It!   Report on a monkey that was let out of its cage by mistake. Use as many words as you can from the Word List on page 54.

Latin Roots

for Word Wisdom

In the News:
The Missing Doughnuts

We've all heard news reports on television. Now, read this transcript, or written record, of a fictional news report.

This is James Laney reporting for WXYZ news. I'm here with Mr. I. M. Clever, Private Detective. We're at Wilco's Corner Bake Shop on Main Street, at the **crossroad** of First Avenue. Mr. Clever, what's the story here?

Mr. Clever: It all started three months ago. Miss Johnson, a bake shop employee, called me with a mystery. Every day a doughnut was missing when the store opened.

Mr. Laney: Interesting. What else did she say?

Mr. Clever: Miss Johnson asked me to **establish** a lookout. She wanted to catch the thief.

Mr. Laney: Interesting. What did you do?

Mr. Clever: Every morning, I would **occupy** a booth at the diner across the street and watch the shop. I had a great view. I was ready to **intercept** the thief.

Mr. Laney: Interesting. What did you see from the diner?

Mr. Clever: Mr. Wilco, the shop's owner, crossed the street in the **crosswalk**. He entered the store at 6 A.M. This happened every day

for two months. It was a **static** routine. Then Mr. Wilco was gone. He disappeared for one week.

Mr. Laney: Interesting. Where did he go?

Mr. Clever: He went on a **cruise** to Alaska. It sounds lovely.

Mr. Laney: Yes, it does. But how did the police get involved?

Mr. Clever: When Mr. Wilco was gone, there was no stealing. I thought the thief wanted to bother Mr. Wilco. I knew that when he returned, the thief would return. This morning, I hid in the store with a video camera. I held the camera **steady** when the back door opened at 6 A.M. I saw a hand reach for the doughnut. Then I dropped the camera, and the man ran away. I **chased** him across the street and tackled him. That's when someone called the police.

Mr. Laney: Interesting. So who was the thief?

Mr. Clever: It was Mr. Wilco! He eats a doughnut for breakfast every morning! The police **arrested** me for attacking Mr. Wilco. Luckily, Miss Johnson explained everything. We all had a good laugh.

Mr. Laney: Interesting. Thank you, Mr. Clever. This is James Laney reporting for WXYZ news.

Practice the Context Clues Strategy Here is one of the boldfaced words from the transcript on page 56. Use the context clues strategy you learned in Part 1 on page 51 to figure out the meaning of this word.

crossroad

Read the sentence that uses the word *crossroad*. Read some of the sentences around the word.

Look for context clues to the word's meaning. Which words tell you **What Kind of Thing the Word Is**?

_____

_____

_____

Think about the context clues. What other helpful information do you know?

_____

_____

_____

Predict a meaning for the word *crossroad*.

_____

_____

_____

Check your Word Wisdom Dictionary to be sure of the meaning of the word *crossroad*. Write the definition here.

_____

_____

_____

Unlock the Meanings

Many English words are made from Latin roots. If you know the meaning of different roots, you can unlock the meaning of many new words. Several words you learned in Part 1 have a Latin root. Each root is related to movement.

Latin Root: **sta**	Latin Root: **cap, cept**	Latin Root: **cruc**
meaning: to stand	meaning: to take, to seize	meaning: cross
English word: *stationary*	English word: *capture*	English word: *across*
meaning: not moving	meaning: to take by force and hold as a prisoner	meaning: from one side to the other

WORD LIST

- crossroad
- establish
- occupy
- intercept
- crosswalk
- static
- cruise
- steady
- chase
- arrest

Sort the Words   Sort the words from the Word List by the letters they begin with. If you can find a root in a word, circle it. When you look for the root *cruc*, also look for *cru* or *cro*. These are other spellings for the root *cruc*.

Words beginning with a vowel

_____
_____
_____
_____

Words beginning with *cr*

_____
_____
_____

Words beginning with other letters

_____
_____
_____

Movement

58 Movement Part 2

Prefix	Meaning
inter-	between

Example

inter- (between) + **cept** (take) = **intercept**

Use Roots and Prefixes Circle any roots and prefixes you find in the boldfaced words. Use roots, prefixes, and context clues to write the meaning of each word.

1 When my dog started to run away from me, I had to **chase** him.

_____

2 Your chair is wobbly. Try sitting on this **steady** chair instead.

_____

3 When my family goes to a movie, we **occupy** four seats in the theater.

_____

4 My parents enjoyed going from port to port on their Alaskan **cruise**.

_____

5 At the **crossroad**, we will turn right onto the main road.

_____

6 For now, Ben's health is **static**; it's not getting better or worse.

_____

7 My teacher **established** a corner of our classroom for silent reading.

_____

8 The police officer will **arrest** the burglar and put him in jail.

_____

9 Amy **intercepted** the ball to stop the other team from scoring.

_____

10 You should cross the busy street only at the **crosswalk**.

_____

WORD LIST

- crossroad
- establish
- occupy
- intercept
- crosswalk
- static
- cruise
- steady
- chase
- arrest

Complete the Word Group   Each set of words has the SAME or ALMOST THE SAME meaning. Write a word from the Word List to complete each group.

1 firm, not shaking, _____

2 run after, follow, _____

3 set up, create, _____

4 interrupt, cut off, _____

5 capture, imprison, _____

Choose the Correct Word   Write the word from the Word List that best completes each sentence.

6 Which way do we go when we get to the

_____?

7 While we were on the _____, we ate our

meals in the ship's dining room.

8 The population in the big city is never

_____. It keeps growing.

9 We walked safely across the street at the

_____.

10 My aunt and uncle _____ the apartment

on the second floor.

Demonstrate Word Knowledge Follow the directions below.

1 Explain the purpose of a **crosswalk**.

_____

2 Name three things that do not remain **static**.

_____

3 Name an outdoor game in which you **chase** someone.

_____

4 Tell what you would do if all the bus seats were **occupied**.

_____

5 Name three things that you need a **steady** hand for.

_____

6 Name a game in which a ball is **intercepted**.

_____

7 Explain what a **crossroad** is.

_____

8 Tell what a school might **establish** to help hungry people.

_____

9 Tell why the police might **arrest** someone.

_____

10 Explain how you are traveling if you are on a **cruise**.

_____

Speak It! Describe something that happened in or near your school last week. Use as many words as you can from the Word List on page 60.

Reference Skills

Moving Through Air:

The Sport of Diving

In seventeenth-century Europe, gymnastics was a very popular sport. During the hot summer months, gymnasts moved their training from the gym to the beach. Here, they began to practice their acrobatics over the water. And this is how the sport of diving began.

From those European beaches, excitement for this new sport spread all over the world. Diving even became an Olympic event in 1904. Let's take a closer look.

There are two main kinds of diving: platform and springboard. A platform diver jumps off of a surface that remains still. The platform does not bounce or **budge**. The platform is thirty-three feet above the water. A springboard is just as it sounds. It is a surface that springs, or bounces, when you jump off of it. The springboard is nearly ten feet above the water.

First, the diver **approaches** the platform or springboard. Then he or she **scales** the ladder to the top. Once on the board, there is little room to **roam** around. He or she must prepare to **deliver** a great dive. If the diver is participating in a competition, judges sit down below. They judge the quality of the dive.

Divers begin in one of three basic ways: They can run to the edge, stand on the edge, or do a handstand on the edge. Instead of running, the diver may **stride** quickly and then jump off the edge. If the diver begins at the edge, he or she usually **departs** the board without bouncing. No matter what, a diver cannot **lurch** forward. All of the movements must be smooth and graceful.

There are many things a diver can do before **plunging** into the water. While in the air, he or she can stay straight, twist, spin, or flip. But this motion is not all the diver is judged on.

Judges watch the diver on the board, in the air, and in the water. Each part of the dive should be graceful. The diver should make little splash when he or she enters the water. At this point the judging is over. The diver can **strut** to the sideline to await the score.

Diving takes a lot of practice and hard work. Maybe you would like to become a great diver. You might even win an Olympic medal someday!

Practice the Context Clues Strategy Here is one of the boldfaced words from the essay on page 62. Use the context clues strategy you learned in Part 1 on page 51 to figure out the meaning of this word.

scale

Read the sentence that uses the word *scale*. Read some of the sentences around the word.

Look for context clues to the word's meaning. Which words tell you **What Kind of Thing the Word Is**?

_____

_____

_____

Think about the context clues. What other helpful information do you know?

_____

_____

_____

Predict a meaning for the word *scale*.

_____

_____

_____

Check your Word Wisdom Dictionary to be sure of the meaning of the word *scale*. Which of the meanings for the word *scale* fits the context?

_____

_____

_____

Guide Words   You know that a dictionary is arranged in ABC (alphabetical) order. To help you find a word you're looking for, dictionaries have guide words. You'll find two guide words on the top of every dictionary page. The first guide word tells you the *first* word on that dictionary page. The second guide word tells you the *last* word on that page.

Guide Words

road   rose

The word *robe* would be on the same page as these guide words. That is because the word *robe* comes between *road* and *rose* in ABC order.

Use Guide Words   Look at each set of guide words. Below the guide words are three words. Which word belongs on the page with those guide words? Circle the word.

1 Guide words: **defeat, den**

depart   deliver   drip

2 Guide words: **say, seal**

strut   stride   scale

3 Guide words: **bubble, call**

approach   budge   can

4 Guide words: **long, meant**

lurch   plunge   mirror

5 Guide words: **river, rope**

scale   route   roam

Find the Meaning

1. Use context clues.
2. Look for a familiar root, prefix, or suffix.
3. If the context or a word part doesn't help, check the dictionary.

Define the Words Follow the steps above to write the meaning of each boldfaced word. Write 1, 2, or 3 to show which steps you used.

1 I tried to move the heavy rock, but it wouldn't **budge**.

_____

2 The train **departs** from the depot at noon and arrives at 1:00 p.m.

_____

3 Look at that peacock. Watch the way it **struts** around the field.

_____

4 When we have nothing to do, Mom and I **roam** around the park.

_____

5 I waited for the letter carrier to **deliver** the letter to me.

_____

6 The climber **scaled** the mountain until she reached the top.

_____

7 Jake bounced off the diving board and **plunged** into the pool.

_____

8 He gave the wagon a quick push, and it **lurched** forward.

_____

9 If I'm in a hurry to get to school, I **stride** down the street.

_____

10 When June **approaches**, we get excited about summer.

_____

WORD LIST
budge
approach
scale
roam
deliver
stride
depart
lurch
plunge
strut

Process the Meanings

WORD LIST

budge
approach
scale
roam
deliver
stride
depart
lurch
plunge
strut

Choose the Correct Word Circle the word in each pair that best completes each sentence. Then write that word on the line. An ending has been added to some of the words.

1 Spying a fish, the seagull _____ into the water. **plunged, delivered**

2 The window was stuck. It wouldn't _____. **strut, budge**

3 To speak to the librarian, just _____ him. **depart, approach**

4 The newspaper is _____ to the front door. **delivered, scaled**

5 This dog used to be shy, but now she _____ around. **struts, plunges**

6 We waved good-bye as the ship _____. **lurched, departed**

7 Hold on! This carnival ride will _____ forward. **lurch, deliver**

8 Sam's long legs allow him to _____ faster than I do. **budge, stride**

9 Watch the squirrel _____ that tall tree. **scale, deliver**

10 Some people love to _____ around museums. **roam, plunge**

Apply What You've Learned

Find Examples   Each word is followed by a sentence. If the sentence is an example of the word, write **yes**. If the sentence is not an example of the word, write **no**.

1 roam   _____ You wander around the park.

2 stride   _____ You skip and hop across the lawn.

3 depart   _____ You come home from your vacation.

4 budge   _____ You can just slightly move a heavy box.

5 plunge   _____ You dive into the pool.

6 deliver   _____ You bring the newspaper to your neighbor.

Relate the Meanings   Answer the questions below.

7 Why would someone **strut** around? _____

_____

8 What happens when you're riding in a car and it **lurches**? _____

_____

9 Who is an easy person to **approach**? Why? _____

_____

10 What is something that people **scale**? _____

_____

Write It! Write sentences combining words from the Word List on page 66. Example: We **roamed** around the park until we **approached** a nice area where we could eat our picnic lunch.

Review

for Word Wisdom

WORD LIST

- compass
- route
- across
- capture
- release
- glide
- soar
- cluster
- stationary
- ascend
- crossroad
- establish
- occupy
- intercept
- crosswalk
- static
- cruise
- steady
- chase
- arrest
- budge
- approach
- scale
- roam
- deliver
- stride
- depart
- lurch
- plunge
- strut

Sort by Syllables and Find Roots Look at each word in the Word List. Count the number of syllables in the word. Write the word in the correct column of the chart.

Then study each word. Look for the roots *sta* (to stand), *cap* or *cept* (to take, to seize), and *cruc* (cross). When you look for the root *cruc*, also look for *cru* or *cro*. These are other spellings for the root *cruc*. If a word has one of those roots, circle the root.

Words with one syllable	Words with two syllables	Words with more than two syllables

Demonstrate Word Knowledge Answer each
question below. Write the correct boldfaced word on the line.

1 Would you **budge** or **plunge** into a pool? _____

2 Would you **lurch** or **scale** a steep hill? _____

3 Would you **stride** or **roam** across a crosswalk?

_____

4 Would you **intercept** or **occupy** a football? _____

5 Would you **glide** or **release** on roller skates? _____

6 Would you **arrest** or **capture** a hamster that got out of its cage?

_____

7 Would your friends **cluster** around or **strut** around a puppet show?

_____

8 Would you **ascend** or **establish** in an elevator?

_____

9 Would you hold your hand **static** or **steady** when you're pouring a

glass of juice? _____

10 When you end a cruise, do you **approach** or **depart** the ship?

_____

Review

Taking Vocabulary Tests

TEST-TAKING STRATEGY
Some tests ask you to find words that are the same or that are close in meaning. After reading the given word, read all the answer choices. Look for the answer choice that is the same or almost the same as the meaning you thought of. Fill in the circle that is next to your answer choice.

Sample:
steady
○ rough in spots
○ long
◉ firm in place
○ dark

Practice Test   Fill in the circle of the answer that is CLOSEST to the meaning of the word.

1 roam
○ enjoy
○ skip
○ jump
○ wander

2 depart
○ arrive
○ leave
○ visit
○ stop

3 release
○ carry
○ keep
○ free
○ rise

4 intercept
○ stop
○ fall
○ tumble
○ race

5 static
○ colorful
○ unchanging
○ moving
○ flickering

6 scale
○ dig
○ climb
○ leap
○ fall

7 route
○ lake
○ plant
○ way
○ map

8 soar
○ turn
○ jump
○ drop
○ fly

9 stationary
○ jumpy
○ still
○ high
○ active

10 stride
○ walk
○ stand
○ sail
○ dance

Add Suffixes A **suffix** is a word ending. When a suffix is added to the end of a word, the suffix usually changes the part of speech of the word. Here is an example.

Part of Speech: verb	Suffix: -ion	Part of Speech: noun
act	act + ion	action

Add a suffix to change each vocabulary word here from a verb to a noun. You will also have to change a letter in one word. Write each new word. Then write a sentence using each new word.

Verb	+ Suffix	= New Word	Sentence
deliver	-y		
establish	-ment		
depart	-ure		
occupy	-ation		
intercept	-or		

Speak It! Tell about ten things you could do outside on a nice day. Use words from the Word List on page 68. Begin each idea this way: "I could . . ." Here is an example: "I could glide on a scooter." Be creative!

PART
1

Context Clues

for Word Wisdom

Bug Eaters:
The Venus Flytrap

The Venus flytrap is a truly amazing plant. While insects usually eat plants, the Venus flytrap is a plant that eats insects. Read this article to find out more.

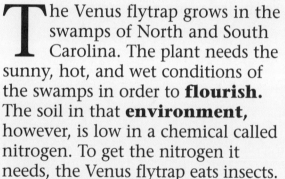

Living Things

The Venus flytrap grows in the swamps of North and South Carolina. The plant needs the sunny, hot, and wet conditions of the swamps in order to **flourish.** The soil in that **environment,** however, is low in a chemical called nitrogen. To get the nitrogen it needs, the Venus flytrap eats insects.

The Venus flytrap has a few **stalks** with leaves at the tip. The leaves smell sweet, and the sweet smell attracts insects. Each leaf is a trap. The leaf has two parts that look like jaws. When an insect lands on a leaf, tiny hairs make the leaf snap shut. The ends come together to make a cage. If you fold your hands and your fingers together, you'll have an idea of what the closed trap is like.

When a trapped insect tries to **escape,** the leaf tightens around it. Then the leaf produces juice to **digest** the insect. Digestion takes five to twelve days. After that, the trap opens. Only the insect's tiny skeleton is left. It will wash away or blow away.

If you put your finger or a pebble on a Venus flytrap, it will also shut. It will not shut tightly, though. Only when a live ant, fly, or any bug moves around inside the trap does the leaf sense a **creature** and tighten its grip. Each time the trap closes, it takes a lot of energy from the plant. After the leaf shuts a few times, the leaf dies. You know the leaves are dying when they droop, or **wilt,** and turn black.

To grow a Venus flytrap of your own, plant it in a glass container with a small opening. Give it lots of sun. Keep it warm and moist. It must have these conditions to **survive.** If you're growing the plant outside, watch out for grasshoppers and caterpillars. These **pests** will eat the leaves. If the plant becomes **infested** with any type of insect, put the plant underwater for a day or two. That will kill all the pests. Although the Venus flytrap is hard to grow at home, it can be done. This bug eater is a very interesting plant to watch.

UNIT
4

Context Clues Strategy

Look for Words Related to the Word

EXAMPLE: The cactus, the sand, and the heat were signs that we were in the *desert*.

CLUE: The words *cactus, sand,* and *heat* are related to the word *desert* and help explain its meaning.

Here is another strategy for using context clues to understand new words. Here, we look at the word *creature,* from the article about the Venus flytrap.

Read the sentence with the unknown word. Read a sentence or two around it.

Only when a live ant, fly, or any bug moves around inside the trap does the leaf sense a **creature** *and tighten its grip.*

Look for context clues. What **Words Related to the Word** can you find?

The words *live ant, fly, or any bug* are related to the word *creature.*

Think about the context clues and other information you may already know.

Ants, flies, and all bugs are living things.

Predict a meaning for the word.

The word *creature* must mean "a living being."

Check the Word Wisdom Dictionary to be sure of the meaning.

A *creature* is a living being, especially an animal.

🔑 Unlock the Meanings

Practice the Strategy   Here is another boldfaced word from the article about the Venus flytrap on page 72. Use the context clues strategy on page 73 to figure out the meaning of the word.

environment

📖 **Read** the sentence that uses the word *environment*. Read some of the sentences around the word.

🔍 **Look** for context clues to the word's meaning. What **Words Related to the Word** can you find?

_____

_____

_____

💡 **Think** about the context clues. What other helpful information do you know?

_____

_____

_____

➡ **Predict** a meaning for the word *environment*.

_____

_____

_____

✔ **Check** your Word Wisdom Dictionary to be sure of the meaning of the word *environment*. Write the definition here.

_____

_____

_____

WORD LIST

flourish

✔ environment

stalk

escape

digest

✔ creature

wilt

survive

pest

infest

Use Context Clues   The two vocabulary words that you have learned from the article are checked off in the Word List. In the first column, write the other eight words from the the Word List. Use context clues to predict a possible meaning for each word in the second column. Then check the meanings in the Word Wisdom Dictionary. Write the dictionary definition in the third column.

Vocabulary Word	Your Prediction	Dictionary Says
1		
2		
3		
4		
5		
6		
7		
8		

Process the Meanings

WORD LIST

flourish
environment
stalk
escape
digest
creature
wilt
survive
pest
infest

Use the Words Correctly in Writing Rewrite each sentence in your own words. Use the word in parentheses in your sentence. You may add an ending to the word.

1 Tomato plants do well with lots of sun. (flourish)

_____

2 Ants are crawling all over the picnic table. (infest)

_____

3 These flowers are starting to bend over. (wilt)

_____

4 The chameleon is a mysterious animal that changes color. (creature)

_____

5 The bird got free from its cage. (escape)

_____

6 These fish can live only in salt water. (environment)

_____

7 Wearing the life preserver saved my life. (survive)

_____

8 The leaves grow from the main part of the plant. (stalk)

_____

9 Your stomach breaks down the food you eat. (digest)

_____

10 Bees may annoy people who are eating outside. (pest)

_____

Apply What You've Learned

Demonstrate Word Knowledge Follow the directions below.

1 Name two kinds of **creatures**.

_____

2 Name two examples of insect or animal **pests**.

_____

3 Name something that will make a plant **flourish**.

_____

4 Tell how a zebra could **escape** from a lion.

_____

5 Name two foods that you **digested** yesterday.

_____

6 Name an **environment** where people can't live.

_____

7 Name something that grows from a **stalk**.

_____

8 Name three things you can't **survive** without.

_____

9 Name something that **wilts**.

_____

10 Name an animal that could **infest** a person's home.

_____

Write It! Write an advertisement for a product that gets rid of pests. Use as many words as you can from Part 1.

Latin Roots

for Word Wisdom

Living Against the Odds:

Desert Plants

Picture a cactus in your mind. Do you see it standing tall surrounded by a desert? This is an accurate picture. But cacti are not the only plants that live in the desert.

We know that jungles are full of plants and flowers. There are lush, green carpets of plants. There are thick, healthy trees and vines. These plants live on rich soil and abundant rains. But plants in the desert have neither of these things. So, how do they survive?

All plants need water to live, just like all other living things. They also take **vitamins** and other nutrients from the soil. These things are **vital** for a plant to stay alive. But a desert is very dry. The soil does not always give a plant the important things it needs to survive. Some desert flowers may look like **inanimate** objects, but they are alive—they have learned to live in this harsh world.

We know that the cactus is one kind of desert plant. A desert cactus waits all year for the rainy season when it rains very heavily. Then, the cactus takes in all the water it can. It uses this water and sunlight to **create** its own food, just like other plants do. But other plants get to do this more than once a year!

Some kinds of shrubs also live in the desert. One kind is called the creosote bush. Scientists think this plant can live for two years without rain. It might get weak, but then a good rain will **revive** it. This plant grows in a neat way. It gets bigger through the **creation** of new branches, or shoots. These new shoots form a ring around the first bush. Some of these bushes can live for thousands of years!

Many desert plants are also **flowering** plants. Some cacti produce beautiful white flowers. The saguaro cactus gives off a very sweet **floral** scent. The creosote bush makes pretty yellow flowers.

If you want to see desert plants, you do not have to go to a real desert. Some **florists** can make a desert world through **animation** that brings a desert to life in an indoor space. The florists keep a room very dry and warm. The plants think they are in a desert. But if you do visit these plants in their natural desert environment, just remember to take lots of water—you're not a cactus!

Practice the Context Clues Strategy Here is one of the boldfaced words from the essay on page 78. Use the context clues strategy you learned in Part 1 on page 73 to figure out the meaning of this word.

vital

Read the sentence that uses the word *vital*. Read some of the sentences around the word.

Look for context clues to the word's meaning. What **Words Related to the Word** can you find?

_____

_____

_____

Think about the context clues. What other helpful information do you know?

_____

_____

Predict a meaning for the word *vital*.

_____

_____

Check your Word Wisdom Dictionary to be sure of the meaning of the word *vital*. Which of the meanings for *vital* fits the context?

_____

_____

Unlock the Meanings

The main part of most English words is called the root. In this lesson you will learn four Latin roots. Each one has something to do with living things.

Latin Root: flor
meaning: flower
English word: *flourish*
meaning: to grow well

Latin Root: vita, viv
meaning: life
English word: *survive*
meaning: to continue to live or exist

Latin Root: anima
meaning: soul, mind
English word: *animated*
meaning: lively

Latin Root: crea
meaning: to create
English word: *creature*
meaning: a living being

Sort by Roots Sort the words from the Word List by their roots. Write each word under the correct root. (One word doesn't have the root *flor*, but it has the word *flower*.) Think of other words you know that come from the same Latin roots. Write each word under the correct root.

WORD LIST

vitamin
vital
inanimate
create
revive
creation
flowering
floral
florist
animation

Latin Root: **flor**

Latin Root: **vita, viv**

Latin Root: **anima**

Latin Root: **crea**

Prefix	Meaning
in-	not

Example

in- (not) + **animate** (alive) = **inanimate**

Use Roots and Prefixes Circle any root and prefix you find in the boldfaced words below. Use context clues, roots, and prefixes to write the meaning of each word.

1 Fruits and vegetables have **vitamins** that we need to stay healthy.

_____

2 I used clay to **create** this bowl.

_____

3 My grandmother buys fresh flowers at the **florist**.

_____

4 This duck looks so real. I didn't realize it was **inanimate**.

_____

5 Exercise is **vital** for good health.

_____

6 We used many art supplies to make a special **creation**.

_____

7 In the center of each table is a colorful **floral** bouquet.

_____

8 After the doctor **revived** the woman, she started to breathe.

_____

9 Her **animation** made us excited about the idea, too.

_____

10 This **flowering** tree has pretty pink petals.

_____

Process the Meanings

WORD LIST

vitamin
vital
inanimate
create
revive
creation
flowering
floral
florist
animation

Replace the Underlined Words Write the best word from the Word List to take the place of the underlined words in each sentence. You may need to add an ending to a word.

1 In science class, we will <u>make</u> a model of a volcano.

_____

2 Rick expresses himself with such <u>cheerful excitement</u>.

_____

3 This plant is wilting, but it can be <u>brought back to</u>

<u>life</u>. _____

4 Studying is <u>very important</u> if we want good grades.

_____

5 We walked in the park and looked at the <u>blossoming</u> trees.

_____

Choose the Correct Word Write the word from the Word List that best completes each sentence. You may need to add an ending to a word.

6 You can buy beautiful bouquets at this

_____ shop.

7 Rocks are _____ objects.

8 This painted pot is a _____ of mine.

9 The roses and tulips were made into a pretty

_____ arrangement.

10 An avocado is a fruit that contains many

_____.

Apply What You've Learned

Demonstrate Word Knowledge Answer the questions below.

1 What is something a **florist** sells?

_____

2 What are two examples of **inanimate** things?

_____

3 What can you **create** with musical instruments?

_____

4 What is something that might have a **floral** design?

_____

5 What is a **creation** that you can make from paper?

_____

Complete the Sentences Write an ending for each sentence.

6 You feel **revived** in the morning if _____

_____

7 You can tell that a tree is **flowering** if _____

8 **Vitamins** help people _____

9 You can see the crowd's **animation** at a ball game when _____

_____

10 Water is **vital** for _____

Speak It! Play a guessing game with a partner. Say, "I'm thinking of . . . ." Use a word from the Word List in Part 2. For example, you might say, "I'm thinking of something **inanimate**." See if your partner can guess what you're thinking of. Give clues if necessary.

PART 3 Reference Skills

Birds of Prey:

Hunters in the Sky

Have you ever seen a bird soaring through the sky in circles? You probably saw a bird of prey. It might have been hunting for its dinner.

There are birds all around us. In our backyards, we might see sparrows, cardinals, and blue jays. We might even feed these birds seeds and fruits. But not all birds are interested in what we put in a birdfeeder. Some birds hunt other animals for their meals.

We study **biology** to learn more about living things. A **zoologist** studies animals very closely. He or she may watch an animal in its **natural** home. Or he or she may **dissect** a dead animal to study its insides. We learn about all kinds of animals from these scientists.

Some birds are called birds of **prey**. This means that they kill living things in order to eat them. The victim is the prey. The animal that kills it is the **predator**. Eagles, hawks, falcons, and buzzards are examples of birds of prey. These birds eat tiny **organisms** like bees and snails. Some eat larger animals like rats and rabbits. Certain falcons even eat other kinds of birds.

Many birds of prey **exist** in forest areas. Some live near lakes, rivers, and oceans. Ospreys and some eagles like to dine on fish. They can fly above water and catch a fish in their claws. Other birds of prey live near fields and grasslands. Some hawks like to eat mice and gophers.

Vultures are a different kind of bird of prey. They do not hunt live animals very often. They mostly eat animals that are already dead. Some of these birds do not have very sharp beaks. They cannot rip through the tough skin of some animals. So, they wait until the animal starts to **decompose**. This makes the skin softer. Most vultures have a keen sense of smell. This helps them to locate the rotting animal bodies.

Killing animals for food is normal, even within the animal kingdom. And it's normal for humans, too. We depend on **agriculture** for much of our food, but most of us eat more than just plants. We also eat other animals. However, while many people do hunt for their food, most of us simply go to the nearest grocery store!

Practice the Context Clues Strategy Here is one of the boldfaced words from the essay on page 84. Use the context clues strategy you learned in Part 1 on page 73 to figure out the meaning of this word.

decompose

Read the sentence that uses the word *decompose*. Read some of the sentences around the word.

Look for context clues to the word's meaning. What **Words Related to the Word** can you find?

_____

_____

Think about the context clues. What other helpful information do you know?

_____

_____

Predict a meaning for the word *decompose*.

_____

_____

Check your Word Wisdom Dictionary to be sure of the meaning of the word *decompose*. Write the definition here.

_____

_____

Base Words A base word is the main part of a word. For example, in the word *existed,* the base word is *exist.* If you look for the word *existed* in the dictionary, you might have a hard time finding it. You have to look up the base word *exist.* A shorter base word will often help you find longer words that are related to it. Here is a dictionary entry for the base word *exist.* Notice that other forms of the word *exist* also appear in the entry.

ex•ist /ĭg zĭst′/ *v.* **ex•ist•ed, ex•ist•ing, ex•ists.** to be alive. *Some plants cannot exist in cold climates.*

Choose the Base Word Look at each pair of words. Circle the word that is the base word.

1 prey   preying

2 dissect   dissecting

3 organisms   organism

4 agricultural   agriculture

5 decompose   decomposed

Write the Base Word Write the base word for each longer word below. You will have to change some endings.

6 creation   _____

7 living   _____

8 discovered   _____

9 scientists   _____

10 hibernation   _____

Find the Meaning

1. Use context clues.
2. Look for a familiar root, prefix, or suffix.
3. If the context or a word part doesn't help, check the dictionary.

Define the Word Follow the three steps above to write the meaning of each boldfaced word. Write 1, 2, or 3 to show which steps you used.

WORD LIST

| biology |
| zoologist |
| natural |
| dissect |
| prey |
| predator |
| organism |
| exist |
| decompose |
| agriculture |

1 To learn about the plant, scientists **dissected** it with a knife.

_____

2 We depend on **agriculture** for some of the foods we eat.

_____

3 A **zoologist** knows the difference between horses and zebras.

_____

4 Bacteria help dead plants **decompose**.

_____

5 The spider caught its **prey** in a large web.

_____

6 This beautiful lake is **natural**; it was not dug out by machines.

_____

7 People cannot **exist** on the moon without special equipment.

_____

8 Birds and cats are dangerous **predators** to a mouse.

_____

9 An ant is an example of a very small **organism**.

_____

10 In our science unit on **biology**, we learned about living things.

_____

Process the Meanings

WORD LIST

- biology
- zoologist
- natural
- dissect
- prey
- predator
- organism
- exist
- decompose
- agriculture

Choose the Correct Word Write the word from the Word List that best completes each sentence. Use each word only once. You will have to add an ending to some words.

1 This pile of leaves will eventually decay and rot, or

_____.

2 On the nature walk, we saw deer, birds, and lots of small,

friendly _____.

3 Many smaller fish must beware of dangerous

_____, like sharks.

4 We are going to learn about the human body in

_____ class.

5 The owl caught its _____ and ate it.

6 A farmer's work has to do with _____.

7 A person must breathe air to _____.

8 You should ask a _____ about that

koala bear.

9 The students watched their science teacher

_____ the dead worm.

10 This red paint is _____; it comes from

berries.

Apply What You've Learned

Solve the Riddles   Write the best word from the Word List for each clue below.

1 I'm hunted and eaten unless I escape. _____

2 My job is to study animals. _____

3 I'm any creature, big or small. _____

4 I'm hunting for my next meal. _____

5 I'm the study of living things. _____

Demonstrate Word Knowledge   Answer the questions below.

6 What's something you need to **exist**? _____

7 What's something that **decomposes**? _____

8 What's something **agriculture** depends on? _____

9 What's something **natural** that you find outside?

_____

10 What's something you'll see if you **dissect** a fish?

_____

Write It!   Write about something in nature that interests you. Use as many words as you can from the Word List on page 88.

PART 4

Review

for Word Wisdom

WORD LIST

- flourish
- environment
- stalk
- escape
- digest
- creature
- wilt
- survive
- pest
- infest
- vitamin
- vital
- inanimate
- create
- revive
- creation
- flowering
- floral
- florist
- animation
- biology
- zoologist
- natural
- dissect
- prey
- predator
- organism
- exist
- decompose
- agriculture

Sort by Beginning Letters Look at the first letter of each word in the Word List. Write the word in the correct column of the chart.

Then study each word. Look for the roots *flor* (flower); *vita, viv* (life); *anima* (soul, mind); and *crea* (to create). If a word has one of those roots, circle the root.

Words beginning with a–d	Words beginning with e–o	Words beginning with p–z

Match the Words Match each vocabulary word with the group of words it goes with best. Write the letter of the matching group on the line.

1 infest _____

2 flourish _____

3 dissect _____

4 create _____

5 environment _____

a. grow, do well, thrive

b. surroundings, natural world, growing conditions

c. make, produce, form

d. crawl all over, swarm, take over

e. cut up, take apart, examine

Demonstrate Word Knowledge Choose the best vocabulary word to answer each question. Write the word on the line.

6 Which word goes with rock? _____

escape   inanimate   creature

7 Which word goes with wolf? _____

predator   vitamin   flowering

8 Which word goes with eating? _____

florist   digest   wilt

9 Which word goes with flower? _____

infest   floral   vitamin

10 Which word goes with excitement? _____

animation   pest   organism

Taking Vocabulary Tests

TEST-TAKING STRATEGY

Always read test directions carefully. Look for words in large type, such as SAME, OPPOSITE, BEST, or MOST. Read all the answers. Then choose the best answer. Here is a sample test item.

Sample:

Fill in the circle of the answer choice that has the SAME meaning as the boldfaced word.

create
- ○ enjoy
- ● make
- ○ eat
- ○ live

Practice Test Fill in the circle of the answer that has the SAME meaning as the boldfaced vocabulary word.

1 vital
- ○ very light
- ○ very dark
- ○ very funny
- ○ very important

2 flourish
- ○ die
- ○ breathe
- ○ grow
- ○ sleep

3 escape
- ○ get away
- ○ eat
- ○ stand still
- ○ live

4 dissect
- ○ wrap around
- ○ cut apart
- ○ tape together
- ○ eat completely

5 decompose
- ○ increase
- ○ rot
- ○ scream
- ○ live

6 exist
- ○ sleep
- ○ get up
- ○ live
- ○ lie down

7 agriculture
- ○ walking
- ○ painting
- ○ building
- ○ farming

8 wilt
- ○ droop
- ○ stand
- ○ water
- ○ bury

9 organism
- ○ a beautiful sky
- ○ a difficult job
- ○ a living thing
- ○ a desk

10 floral
- ○ like insects
- ○ like water
- ○ like air
- ○ like flowers

Play with Language

Solve the Riddles The riddles below are called Hink Pinks. The words in the answer rhyme. Use a word from the Word List on page 90 to solve each Hink Pink. The words in boldface will give you a clue.

1 What do you call an **annoying bug** that comes to your

house uninvited? a _____ guest

2 What do you call a conversation between two flower **stems**?

a _____ talk

3 What do you call a person who teaches **animals**?

a _____ teacher

4 What do you call the "fun" a cat has with a **mouse** before

trying to eat it? _____ play

Unscramble the Words The letters in these vocabulary words are all scrambled. Unscramble them and write the word on the line. Use the Word List on page 90 to help you.

5 gyobiol _____

6 vivree _____

7 etocnari _____

8 naraltu _____

9 vreisuv _____

10 logooztsi _____

Speak It! Imagine that you are taking a nature walk in the forest. Describe out loud what you see. Take turns with your classmates. Use as many words as you can from the Word List on page 90.

PART

1

Context Clues

for Word Wisdom

At Work and Play:

The Game of Monopoly

The game of Monopoly™ is played by people around the world. Maybe you have played it. Read this article to learn how it came about.

According to Parker Brothers, Monopoly began with a man named Charles Darrow. Darrow was **jobless**. He had lost his job in the 1929 stock market crash.

Without work, it was hard to **afford** food and shelter. To pass the time, Darrow invented a new board game about buying and selling property. Each property was named after a street in Atlantic City, New Jersey.

People enjoyed playing the game and spending play money. Darrow started to make game boards for his family and friends. Then he began to sell them. He couldn't **produce** enough games to keep up with the orders.

Darrow then wrote to Parker Brothers, a major game company. Perhaps it would buy the game. Unlike Darrow, who didn't know much about the board-game business, the people at Parker Brothers were **experts**. They liked the game, but felt that the rules were too hard. They also didn't

like the game's **goal**. In other games, the goal was to get around the board first. In Monopoly, the goal was to be the only player left with money.

But Darrow knew his game was a winner. A local department store in Philadelphia agreed to **market** it. Darrow took out a **loan**. With the money he borrowed, he made 5,000 game sets.

Word got back to Parker Brothers that the game was selling fast. Parker Brothers decided to pay Darrow for each Monopoly set sold. In 1935, Parker Brothers was producing 20,000 Monopoly sets every week. But the people at Parker Brothers were afraid that, unlike things that would be around for a long time, Monopoly was just a **fad**. They were sure that the game would soon go out of style.

That never happened. Charles Darrow became very **wealthy**. He was the first game **inventor** to become a millionaire. And, Monopoly is still a popular game today.

Context Clues Strategy

Look for What the Word Is Not Like

EXAMPLE: Unlike coins, which are made of metal, *bills* are made of paper.

CLUE: The words *bills* and *coins* are contrasted. That means they are compared in a way that shows how they are different. Bills are not like coins, which are made of metal. That means that bills are not made of metal.

Here is another strategy for using context clues to understand new words.

Read the sentence with the unknown word. Read a sentence or two around it.

Unlike Darrow, who didn't know much about the board-game business, the people at Parker Brothers were **experts**.

Look for context clues. What clues can you find that show **What the Word Is Not Like**?

The words *Unlike Darrow, who didn't know much about* are a clue about what the word *experts* is contrasted with.

Think about the context clues and other information you may already know.

I've heard *experts* used to describe people who know a lot.

Predict a meaning for the word.

Expert must mean "a person who knows a lot about something."

Check the Word Wisdom Dictionary to decide which of the meanings fits the context.

An expert is a person with great knowledge or skill in a particular field.

🔒 Unlock the Meanings

Practice the Strategy The word in the box below is from the article on page 94. Use the context clues strategy on page 95 to figure out the meaning of the word.

fad

📖 **Read** the sentence that uses the word *fad*. Read some of the sentences around the word.

🔍 **Look** for context clues. What clues can you find that show **What the Word Is Not Like?**

_____

_____

_____

💡 **Think** about the context clues. What other helpful information do you already know?

_____

_____

_____

➡ **Predict** a meaning for the word *fad*.

_____

_____

_____

✔ **Check** your Word Wisdom Dictionary to be sure of the meaning of the word *fad*. Write the definition here.

_____

_____

WORD LIST
jobless
afford
produce
✔expert
goal
market
loan
✔fad
wealthy
inventor

Use Context Clues Two words you have learned from the article are checked off in the Word List. In the first column, write the other eight words from the Word List. In the second column, use context clues to predict a meaning for each word. Then look up the meaning of the word in your Word Wisdom Dictionary. In the third column, write the dictionary meaning that fits the context.

	Vocabulary Word	Your Prediction	Dictionary Says
1			
2			
3			
4			
5			
6			
7			
8			

Process the Meanings

WORD LIST

jobless
afford
produce
expert
goal
market
loan
fad
wealthy
inventor

Solve the Riddles Write the word from the Word List that fits each clue.

1 I am a person who thinks up one-of-a-kind things.

_____

2 This is money you have to pay back.

_____

3 I am a person full of knowledge about something.

_____

4 This used to be popular, but it isn't anymore.

_____

5 Someone with a lot of money can be described as this.

_____

Replace the Words Write the word from the Word List that correctly replaces the underlined word or words.

6 My older brother can't find a job. He's <u>out of work</u>.

_____

7 How many eggs can a chicken <u>make</u> in a week?

_____

8 I don't understand the <u>point</u> of this plan.

_____

9 The store will <u>sell</u> the new book. _____

10 I wish I had enough money to <u>pay for</u> a new computer.

_____

Complete the Analogies Choose the word that best completes each sentence. Write your answer on the line.

1 Happy is to sad as **wealthy** is to _____.
a. poor   b. healthy   c. rich   d. mad

2 Buy is to get as **market** is to _____.
a. find   b. eat   c. sell   d. take

3 Poet is to poetry as **inventor** is to _____.
a. write   b. writer   c. invent   d. invention

4 Destroy is to ruin as **produce** is to _____.
a. make   b. throw   c. tear   d. mad

5 Gift is to keep as **loan** is to _____.
a. give   b. return   c. own   d. have

Connect the Words Write a word from the Word List that goes with each phrase.

6 a person who knows more than most about something _____

7 doesn't have paying work _____

8 being able to buy something _____

9 a hairstyle that was popular ten years ago _____

10 the finish line of a race _____

Write It! Imagine that you are a very wealthy person. What do you do with your money? Write about your ideas. Use as many words from the Word List in Part 1 as you can.

PART 2 Latin Roots

for Word Wisdom

A Sweet Dream:
Milton Hershey

What kind of candy do you like best? A lot of people choose chocolate. Did you know that Hershey's™ is the largest maker of chocolate in our country?

Milton Hershey had a huge dream. He wanted to make delicious candy. So he built his own factory. He did **experiments** with chocolate. He came up with **productive** new ideas. He made new machines for his factory. The machines made a lot of candy **products** at once. Because of this, the candy bars did not cost much. The company gave people tasty candy at a low price.

The Pennsylvania town where Hershey built his factory was named after him. Many people moved to the city for jobs. Other businesses started. But it is not just a **commercial** town. Many parts of the city do not have to do with business at all. There are homes and schools. There are hospitals and parks. But the most famous place in town is the Hershey factory!

Chocolate is their area of **expertise**. But the company makes other **merchandise,** too.

They make hard candy and even licorice. But it's the chocolate that people love the most. So just how is this candy made?

Chocolate starts on a tree. From this tree we get cocoa beans. These beans are the first step in the **production** of chocolate. Cocoa beans are sent to the company from around the world. At the factory, the beans are mixed, roasted, and ground up. Some other ingredients, like milk and sugar, are added to the ground beans. A gooey substance forms. This chocolate is poured into a mold to give the candy its shape. Then machines wrap the candy products. They are put in boxes and shipped to **merchants** everywhere.

The company also does some **commerce** in other countries. But most of their business is done in the U.S. Americans really love Hershey's chocolate! We eat it in cookies and cakes. We eat candy bars. We drink it in hot cocoa.

If you ever go to the town of Hershey, visit the factory. You can see for yourself how the candy is made. It will be an **experience** you will not forget. You might even get a free sample!

Practice the Context Clues Strategy   Here is one of the boldfaced words from the essay on page 100. Use the context clues strategy you learned in Part 1 on page 95 to figure out the meaning of this word.

commercial

Read the sentence that uses the word *commercial*. Read some of the sentences around the word.

Look for context clues to the word's meaning. What clues can you find that show **What the Word Is Not Like?**

_____

_____

_____

Think about the context clues. What other helpful information do you know?

_____

_____

_____

Predict a meaning for the word *commercial*.

_____

_____

_____

Check your Word Wisdom Dictionary to be sure of the meaning of the word *commercial*. Which meaning for *commercial* fits the context? Write the definition here.

_____

_____

_____

Many English words come from Latin roots. If you know the meaning of different roots, you can often unlock the meaning of new words. Some words you learned in Part 1 have a Latin root that is related to work and money.

Latin Root: **merc**
meaning: to trade
English word: *market*
meaning: to sell

Latin Root: **exper**
meaning: to try
English word: *expert*
meaning: a person who knows a lot about something

Latin Root: **duc**
meaning: to lead
English word: *produce*
meaning: to make something

WORD LIST

experiment
productive
product
commercial
expertise
merchandise
production
merchant
commerce
experience

Sort by Roots Find the roots you just learned in the Word List. Write each word in the correct column. Then think of other words you know that come from the same Latin roots. Write each word in the correct column.

Latin Root: **merc**

Latin Root: **exper**

Latin Root: **duc**

Work and Money

Prefix	Meaning
com-	with

Example

com- (with) + merce (trade) = commerce

Use Roots and Prefixes Circle any roots and prefixes you find in the boldfaced words below. Use context clues, roots, and prefixes to write the meaning of the word. Check your definitions in the dictionary.

1 This is a **commercial** area with lots of stores.

_____

2 Cheese is a dairy **product**.

_____

3 Our **experiment** proved that oil and water don't mix.

_____

4 This **merchant** sells only shirts and shoes.

_____

5 We cleaned up the attic. It was a **productive** day.

_____

6 Dan is good at art. It is his area of **expertise**.

_____

7 There is no **commerce** today. The stores are closed.

_____

8 When the factory ran out of flour, the **production** of bread stopped.

_____

9 I like this store because it has the best **merchandise**.

_____

10 Riding in a submarine was an amazing **experience**.

_____

WORD LIST

- experiment
- productive
- product
- commercial
- expertise
- merchandise
- production
- merchant
- commerce
- experience

Choose the Correct Words From each pair of words, write the word that best completes each sentence.

1 This downtown _____ sells school supplies. (merchant, production)

2 When we go shopping, my father drives to the _____ district. (commercial, product)

3 Our class did an _____ with electricity, and it worked! (expertise, experiment)

4 Before, these countries traded with each other. Today, there is no _____ between them. (commerce, experience)

5 Now that people listen to CDs, the _____ of tapes has slowed down. (productive, production)

6 Paper is a _____ made from trees. (product, commercial)

7 Mia does well in her math class. Math is her area of _____. (experiment, expertise)

8 Let's not sit and do nothing. Instead, let's be _____. (productive, product)

9 Before that store closed, it sold all of its _____. (commerce, merchandise)

10 Skiing for the first time was a great _____. (expertise, experience)

Apply What You've Learned

Relate the Meanings Write sentences to follow the directions.

1 Give an example of how you can be **productive** at home.

_____

2 Write a sentence about someone's area of **expertise**.

_____

3 Name the type of **merchandise** you enjoy shopping for most.

_____

4 Tell about an interesting **experience** you've had.

_____

5 Explain how you would know if you were in a **commercial** area.

_____

_____

Complete the Sentences Finish each sentence. Write an ending that makes sense.

6 The **experiment** failed because _____

7 There is no **commerce** between the cities because _____

_____

8 If the **production** of postage stamps stopped, _____

_____

9 A **merchant** is happy if _____

10 Two **products** we get from factories are _____

Speak It! Imagine that you could invent a new product. What would it be? Try to sell the product to your class. First, practice with a partner. Use as many words from the Word List in Part 2 as you can.

PART 3 Reference Skills

Working for a Living:

How to Get a Job

Think about the teenagers and adults you know. Many of them probably have jobs. But how did they get those jobs?

Many people do not have a job while they are in school. But they do find **employment** when they graduate from high school or college. Other people begin working early in life. They might deliver newspapers or bag groceries at a local store. Most people have to work at some point in their lives. What will getting a job be like?

Some kinds of **labor** require that you use your muscles. You might mow lawns, trim trees, and plant gardens. You could also **assemble** toys in a factory. On the other hand, you might take apart items at a junkyard or work at a construction site. There are many jobs that demand hard work from your body.

For many jobs you'll need to turn in an **application**. You must **supply** information about yourself on this piece of paper. You write where you live. You tell about your education. You describe other jobs you have had. You can also tell about your special skills. For example, you might be good with computers. Some of your skills might even fit in with certain jobs. If you want to work at a bank, you should note that you are familiar with **currency** from different countries. If you want a job at an auto shop, you should tell about your **mechanical** skills.

But, how do you know if you **qualify** for a job? You might see an ad in the newspaper. It will describe the job. See if your skills match the job. You can also talk to someone at the **organization**. Tell them a little about yourself. Ask them if the job is right for you.

You can learn a new job as an **assistant**. This way you can see how a professional works. You might be an assistant to a lawyer. You will see court cases. You will meet clients. Or you might be an assistant to a chef. You will see what it is like to work in a kitchen. All of this experience will help you decide what job you would like in the future. What job might you be good at?

Practice the Context Clues Strategy Here is one of the boldfaced words from the essay on page 106. Use the context clues strategy you learned in Part 1 on page 95 to figure out the meaning of this word.

assemble

Read the sentence that uses the word *assemble*. Read some of the sentences around the word.

Look for context clues to the word's meaning. What clues can you find that show **What the Word Is Not Like?**

_____

_____

_____

Think about the context clues. What other helpful information do you know?

_____

_____

_____

Predict a meaning for the word *assemble*.

_____

_____

_____

Check your Word Wisdom Dictionary to be sure of the meaning of the word *assemble*. Write the definition here.

_____

_____

_____

Dictionary Definitions: Multiple Meanings

Some words have more than one meaning. Each meaning may be listed in a separate dictionary entry that is numbered. The number comes after the word.

Dictionaries use labels to tell what part of speech a word is. The letter *n.* stands for *noun.* The letter *v.* stands for *verb.* Sometimes a dictionary will tell how to spell the plural form of a noun. The letters *pl.* stand for *plural.*

Here are three dictionary entries for the word *supply*:

sup•ply[1] /sə plī′/ *v.* **sup•plied, sup•ply•ing, sup•plies.** to give things for people to use; to provide. *Does the school supply students with pencils and paper?*—**sup•pli•er** *n.*
sup•ply[2] /sə plī′/ *v.* **sup•plied, sup•ply•ing, sup•plies.** to make available (to satisfy a need or want). *We can supply your need for extra house keys.*—**sup•pli•er** *n.*
sup•ply[3] /sə plī′/ *n., pl.* **sup•plies.** the amount that is available. *Do we have a large supply of napkins for the party?*

Choose the Correct Definitions Choose the correct definition for the word *supply* in each sentence. Look for the raised number after the first word in each entry above. Write the number on the line.

1 We have a large **supply** of gift boxes if you need some. ____

2 Does this school **supply** tissues for every classroom? ____

3 Our **supply** of cereal is very low, so let's go food shopping. ____

4 Can your teacher **supply** your need for help with today's homework? ____

5 The library **supplies** computer time for everyone. ____

Find the Meaning

1. Use context clues.
2. Look for a familiar root, prefix, or suffix.
3. If the context or a word part doesn't help, check the dictionary.

Define the Words Follow the steps above to write the meaning of each boldfaced word. Then write 1, 2, or 3 to show which steps you used.

WORD LIST

employment

labor

assemble

application

supply

currency

mechanical

qualify

organization

assistant

1 If Terri wins this round, she will **qualify** for the finals.

_____

2 I followed the directions to **assemble** the robot.

_____

3 The doctor needed an **assistant** to help him perform the surgery.

_____

4 My muscles hurt from the **labor** of planting a garden.

_____

5 The dollar is used as American **currency**.

_____

6 My brother can't fix the clock because he has no **mechanical** skills.

_____

7 Can the company **supply** new desks for the school?

_____

8 When Ms. Jones lost her job, she looked for new **employment**.

_____

9 This **organization** delivers food to people who need it.

_____

10 To get a job at this store, you have to fill out an **application**.

_____

WORD LIST

- employment
- labor
- assemble
- application
- supply
- currency
- mechanical
- qualify
- organization
- assistant

Complete the Groups The two words in each group below have related meanings. Write the word from the Word List that belongs in each group.

1 money, coins, _____

2 helper, aide, _____

3 build, construct, _____

4 group, business, _____

5 give, provide, _____

Use the Words Correctly in Writing Rewrite each sentence using the word in parentheses. You may wish to add an ending to the word.

6 Jake filled out a form for a job at the bank. (application)

_____

7 Mrs. Mitchell would like to find work as a nurse. (employment)

_____

8 It takes a lot of effort to build a house. (labor)

_____

9 I'm so glad I could do what I needed to be on the team. (qualify)

_____

10 To fix cars, you need skill in working with machines. (mechanical)

_____

Apply What You've Learned

Review the Meanings Each sentence has a boldfaced word from the Word List. Decide if the sentence is true or false. Write **T** for **true** or **F** for **false** on the line.

_____ **1** If you need to **assemble** a chair, you will take it apart.

_____ **2** A **mechanical** toy would have moving parts.

_____ **3** To **qualify** for the soccer team, you should play badly.

_____ **4** The job of an **assistant** is to be in charge.

_____ **5** An **organization** can be a group that does volunteer work.

_____ **6** A place of **employment** is where someone works.

Show Word Knowledge Choose the correct words to make a true statement. Write your choice on the line.

7 The **currency** of a country is for _____

_____

a. buying and selling things.   b. counting people.   c. finding places.

8 An **application** can help a person _____

a. learn to do a job.   b. lift heavy things.   c. get a job.

9 The **labor** it takes to build a fence is the _____

_____

a. material needed.   b. total cost.   c. work involved.

10 Cows **supply** _____

a. grass.   b. milk.   c. eggs.

Write It! What kind of work would you like to do someday? Write about it. Use some words from the Part 3 Word List.

Review

for
Word
Wisdom

WORD LIST

jobless
afford
produce
expert
goal
market
loan
fad
wealthy
inventor
experiment
productive
product
commercial
expertise
merchandise
production
merchant
commerce
experience
employment
labor
assemble
application
supply
currency
mechanical
qualify
organization
assistant

Sort by First Letter Look at each word in the Word List. Does the word start with a vowel or a consonant? Write the word in the correct column. Then study each word. Look for the roots **merc, exper,** and **duc**. If a word has one of those roots, circle the root.

Words beginning with a vowel	Words beginning with a consonant

Choose the Correct Words Circle the vocabulary word that correctly completes the sentence.

1 When shopping, use (currency, commerce) to pay.

2 To join some clubs, you have to complete an (expertise, application).

3 If a factory has no power, it may have trouble with (experiment, production).

4 If you have the money to buy something, you can (afford, qualify) it.

5 People like to shop at a store with good (merchandise, application).

Answer the Questions Use what you have learned about the boldfaced words to answer the questions. Write **yes** or **no**. Be ready to explain your answers.

_____ **6** Does a **productive organization** get a lot done?

_____ **7** Does a **jobless** person have **employment**?

_____ **8** Would a **merchant** want to sell a toy that was a **fad** five years ago?

_____ **9** If you are an **expert**, do you have **expertise**?

_____ **10** If someone gave you a **loan**, should it be your **goal** to pay it back?

Taking Vocabulary Tests

TEST-TAKING STRATEGY

Always read all the answer choices. Be careful of answer choices that make sense in the sentence but don't have the same meaning as the boldfaced word. Before you pick an answer, replace the boldfaced word with it. See if the sentence has the same meaning.

Sample:

My aunt is **wealthy**.
- ○ smart
- ● rich
- ○ nice
- ○ poor

Practice Test Choose the word or words that mean the same and that could take the place of the boldfaced word in each sentence.

1 Lifting heavy boxes is hard **labor**.
- ○ help
- ○ business
- ○ play
- ○ work

2 My **expertise** is singing.
- ○ skill
- ○ art
- ○ work
- ○ hobby

3 The hike was a great **experience**.
- ○ thing to eat
- ○ thing to do
- ○ thing to buy
- ○ thing to sell

4 I'll **supply** popcorn for the party.
- ○ market
- ○ eat
- ○ trade
- ○ provide

5 The nurse is the doctor's **assistant**.
- ○ teacher
- ○ helper
- ○ coach
- ○ boss

6 She can **afford** a new bike.
- ○ find
- ○ ride
- ○ pay for
- ○ sell

7 Let's **assemble** the train track.
- ○ take apart
- ○ put together
- ○ paint
- ○ sell

8 Jim is **jobless**.
- ○ without a job
- ○ without help
- ○ without food
- ○ without a home

9 Bees **produce** honey.
- ○ eat
- ○ get
- ○ like
- ○ make

10 The store is full of **merchandise**.
- ○ people who shop
- ○ helpful salespeople
- ○ things to buy
- ○ sale signs

Changing Suffixes Changing suffixes can help you make new words. Here is an example.

Word	− Subtract	+ Add	= New Word
application	-ion	-or	= applicator

Do the subtraction and addition below. Write the new words.

Word	− Subtract	+ Add	New Word
assistant	-ant	-ance	
afforded	-ed	-able	
assemble	-e	-y	
employment	-ment	-er	
wealthy	-y	-ier	
productive	-e	-ity	
mechanical	-ical	-ize	
qualify	-y	-ication	
inventor	-or	-ive	
organization	-ation	-er	

Speak It! A business owner is interviewing people who want a job. You want to know more about it. What questions would you ask the owner? What questions might the owner ask you? Find a partner and play the part of the business owner and worker. Ask each other questions. Use several words from the Part 4 Word List.

Context Clues

for Word Wisdom

Speedy Mail Delivery:

The Pony Express

When Abraham Lincoln was elected president in 1860, people in California first learned about it ten days later. In 1860, ten days was fast because of the Pony Express. Read this article to learn more about it.

The Pony Express was a mail delivery service. It operated from 1860 to 1861. **Prior** to the Pony Express, letters to and from California were sent by ship and wagon train. It took months for **news** to reach one end of the country from the other. A faster way of delivering mail was needed. The Pony Express was the answer.

The Pony Express was a business. It promised speedy and **timely** delivery of mail by young men who rode on lightning-fast horses. The route was almost 2,000 miles long from Missouri to California. Riders would cover about 250 miles each day. The **time frame** to complete a trip was eight to twelve days.

The Pony Express trail was an **indefinite** route, not an exact path. Riders had to travel through rough wilderness, deserts, and mountains. Along certain stretches there was no grass or water.

Before the service began, the trail had to be prepared. This was **tedious** work. It took a long time for bridges to be built across many streams. Large rocks had to be removed from roads. Wells had to be dug. Paths through high mountains had to be cleared. The strongest and fastest horses had to be bought. Stations needed to be built so riders and horses could take a rest and eat.

The bravery of the riders made the Pony Express famous. The riders needed courage to face blizzards, desert heat, and outlaws. **Precautions** were used to keep the riders safe. For example, no gold or silver could be carried along. This way, riders would not be robbed by outlaws.

Schedules were used to make sure the mail was delivered on time. In its whole history, the Pony Express lost only one mail delivery.

The Pony Express was put out of business by the **completion** of the telegraph line. With the telegraph, messages that took eight weeks by ship, or eight days by the Pony Express, took only four hours. The **final** ride took place in October 1861.

Time UNIT 6

Context Clues Strategy

Look for What the Word Is Used For

EXAMPLE: The swinging *pendulum* keeps large clocks ticking regularly.

CLUE: The phrase *keeps large clocks ticking regularly* tells what a *pendulum* is used for.

Here is another strategy to figure out the meaning of the word *precautions* from the essay on page 116.

Read the sentence with the unknown word. Read some of the sentences around it.

Precautions were used to keep the riders safe. For example, no gold or silver could be carried along.

Look for context clues. What clues showing **What the Word Is Used For** can you find?

The words *to keep the riders safe* is a clue about what *precautions* are used for.

Think about the context clues and other helpful information you may already know.

Riders couldn't carry gold and silver. That would protect them from being robbed.

Predict a meaning for the word.

Precautions might mean "things to keep something bad from happening."

Check your Word Wisdom Dictionary to be sure of the meaning.

The word *precaution* means "an act to guard against an upcoming event."

🔒 Unlock the Meanings

Practice the Strategy The boldfaced word below is from the article about the Pony Express on page 116. Use the context clues strategy on page 117 to figure out the meaning of the word.

schedules

📖 **Read** the sentence that uses the word *schedules*. Read some of the sentences around the word.

🔍 **Look** for context clues. What clues showing **What the Word Is Used For** can you find?

_____

_____

💡 **Think** about the context clues. What other helpful information do you already know?

_____

_____

➡️ **Predict** a meaning for the word *schedule*.

_____

_____

✔️ **Check** the Word Wisdom Dictionary to be sure of the meaning of the word *schedule*. Which meaning for the word *schedule* fits the context?

_____

_____

WORD LIST
prior
news
timely
time frame
indefinite
tedious
✔ precaution
✔ schedule
completion
final

Use Context Clues You have been introduced to two vocabulary words from the Pony Express article. Those words are checked off in the Word List here. In the first column below, write the other eight words from the Word List. Use context clues to predict a meaning for each word in the second column. Then check the meanings in the Word Wisdom Dictionary. Write the definition in the third column.

	Vocabulary Word	Your Prediction	Dictionary Says
1			
2			
3			
4			
5			
6			
7			
8			

Process the Meanings

WORD LIST

prior

news

timely

time frame

indefinite

tedious

precaution

schedule

completion

final

Choose the Correct Word Write the vocabulary word that best completes each sentence.

1 It seems that this heat wave will last for an

_____ amount of time.

2 Kayla can't go to Alyssa's house because she made

_____ plans with Isabel.

3 Painting this very long fence is _____

work.

4 The school lunch _____ shows that

pizza will be served on Friday.

5 Many people listen to the _____ on

the radio.

6 I'll be done reading this book after I finish the

_____ chapter.

7 What is your _____ for finishing the

social studies report?

8 If we finish our homework in a _____

manner, we can go to the movies.

9 It's wise to keep a flashlight in the car as a safety

_____.

10 After the _____ of the bridge, cars will

be able to cross this river.

Apply What You've Learned

Show Word Knowledge Use what you know about the boldfaced words to answer each question. Write **Yes** or **No**. Then explain your answer.

1 Does a train **schedule** show when trains arrive?

_____

2 Is a **final** test the first one?

_____

3 Is last year's election **news** today?

_____

4 Do you start your science project at its **completion**?

_____

5 Do you want **timely** answers to your questions?

_____

6 Is a **tedious** job something you would enjoy?

_____

7 Did you go to college **prior** to third grade?

_____

8 Can the weather be **indefinite**?

_____

9 Do you take **precautions** before crossing a street?

_____

10 Do you go to school during a certain **time frame**?

_____

 Write It! Pretend you are in charge of a bake sale. Write about your plans and your time frame. Use several Part 1 vocabulary words.

Latin Roots

for Word Wisdom

Protect the Past:
Repairing Old Buildings

Did you ever visit a really old building? Did you wonder what life was like a long time ago? Some buildings can *show* you what the past was like.

We learn a lot from history, so it is important to protect it. We protect history by writing books and by building statues of important people. We also protect history by **renovating** important buildings. This helps a building last for a long time. It also shows us how the building looked a long time ago. The Thomas Jefferson Building is a huge old building in Washington, D.C. that holds the Library of Congress. It tells us a lot about the past.

The government had a contest a long time ago. It asked builders to plan a new building that would serve as a library. Many people sent their plans, but there were only a few **finalists**. In 1873, the judges picked a **definite** winner. The plan did not have any **novel** ideas—the building looked like other buildings of the time. But the judges liked the plan. The building was finished in 1897.

By the 1980s, the Jefferson Building needed to be repaired. The government did not have an **infinite** amount of money to spend. They had to **define** their plans. First, fire alarms and sprinklers were added. This made the building safer. These are things that **contemporary** buildings have. But not all of the changes made the building more modern. The workers tried to make the building look like it did in 1897. They kept many of the old objects in the building. They worked to **renew** some tables from 1897. The tables now look like they did when they were new.

Some rooms had to be closed during the repair, but that was only **temporary**. The rooms reopened when the work was finished. Some **novelties** were added to the building, too. It has some things that it did not have in 1897, like computers.

The Thomas Jefferson Building now shows off the old and the new. You can go there to study and read about history. You can also go there to see history in the building and in its walls, floors, and furniture!

Practice the Context Clues Strategy Here is one of the boldfaced words from the essay on page 122. Use the context clues strategy you learned in Part 1 on page 117 to figure out the meaning of this word.

renovating

Read the sentence that uses the word *renovating*. Read some of the sentences around the word.

Look for context clues. What words show **What the Word Is Used For**?

_____

_____

_____

Think about the context clues. What other helpful information do you know?

_____

_____

Predict a meaning for the word *renovate*.

_____

_____

Check your Word Wisdom Dictionary to be sure of the meaning of the word *renovate*. Write the definition here.

_____

_____

Unlock the Meanings

Many English words come from Latin roots. If you know the meaning of different roots, you can often figure out the meaning of new words. Some of the words you learned in Part 1 have Latin roots. Each root is related to time.

Latin Root: **fin**
meaning: end
English word: *final*
meaning: last

Latin Root: **new, nov**
meaning: new
English word: *news*
meaning: recent information

Latin Root: **temp**
meaning: time
English word: *timely*
meaning: happening at the right time

WORD LIST

renovate

finalist

definite

novel

infinite

define

contemporary

renew

temporary

novelty

Sort by Roots Sort the words in the Word List by their roots. Write each word in the correct column. Then think of other words you know that come from the same Latin roots. Write those words in the correct column.

Time

Latin Root:
fin

Latin Root:
new, nov

Latin Root:
temp

Prefix	Meaning
con-	with

Example

con- (with) + temp (time) + -orary (adj.)
= contemporary

Use Roots and Prefixes Circle the roots and any prefixes you find in the boldfaced words below. Use context clues, roots, and prefixes to write the meaning of each word. Check your definitions in the Word Wisdom Dictionary.

1 If there is lightning, it's **definite** that we can't swim.

_____

2 During a spring shower, the rain is only **temporary**.

_____

3 That was a **novel** idea to make a statue out of old soda cans.

_____

4 After two rounds, I became a **finalist** in the spelling contest.

_____

5 Could you **define** this hard word for me?

_____

6 The owners **renovated** their old house to make it modern.

_____

7 My library card is good for one year. Then I have to **renew** it.

_____

8 Some people like old-fashioned furniture, not **contemporary** styles.

_____

9 When chewing gum was first invented, it was a **novelty**.

_____

10 There seems to be an **infinite** number of stars in the sky.

_____

Process the Meanings

WORD LIST

- renovate
- finalist
- definite
- novel
- infinite
- define
- contemporary
- renew
- temporary
- novelty

Find the Right Words   Read this letter from Dave to his friend Jake. Complete it with words from the Word List.

Dear Jake,

   Hi! I really miss everyone since I moved away. I'm still homesick. I hope these feelings are **1** _____. My dad says they'll go away soon. My new house is really great. It was old, so my parents decided to **2** _____ it. It now has some **3** _____ advantages for me. Now the basement is modern and **4** _____. My mom says that she knew it had endless and **5** _____ possibilities. She was right. It now has a video game center and table tennis! I can't wait until you come for a visit.

                                                  Your friend,
                                                  Dave

Choose the Correct Word   Write the word from the Word List that could replace the underlined words.

6 the <u>player in the last contest</u>   _____

7 <u>restart</u> the subscription   _____

8 quite a <u>new and unusual thing</u>   _____

9 <u>explain the meaning of</u> the word   _____

10 such <u>new and unusual</u> ideas   _____

11 a <u>modern or current</u> design   _____

12 <u>certain</u> plans for vacation   _____

Complete the Sentences Complete each sentence with a word from the Word List. You will have to add an ending to one word.

1 Dan wants to _____ his club membership for another year.

2 The building is closed while it's being _____.

3 I have set a _____ date for my oral report.

4 This is a fresh and _____ plan.

5 Aunt Emily likes modern, _____ jewelry.

Show Word Knowledge Choose the phrase that best completes each sentence. Write the letter of your choice on the line.

6 A **temporary** situation would be _____
    a. waiting at the airport.   b. working for thirty years.

7 Someone with an **infinite** number of fears is most likely _____
    a. a scared person.   b. a calm person.

8 **Finalists** hope to _____
    a. be on the best team.   b. begin a chess contest.

9 A **novelty** is something that _____
    a. people have to survive.   b. people are interested in trying.

10 If I **define** something for you, it's because _____
    a. I want to explain it.   b. I want to give it to you.

Speak It! Find a partner and play a guessing game. Say a clue for each vocabulary word in Part 2. For example, you might think of *library card* to go with *renew*. Have your partner guess the vocabulary word. Then switch roles.

Reference Skills

for Word Wisdom

School Days:

Preparing for the Future

What have you noticed as you grow older? You get taller. Schoolwork gets harder. Life gets more exciting. You have many fun times to look forward to. But there will also be challenges.

When things are new, it's not always comfortable. On the first day of each new school year, it takes some time to get used to things. Then you get into a **routine**. You **eventually** feel comfortable with life again. These **frequent** changes help you "grow up," or become more mature.

Students go from grade school to middle school to high school. Each school year is like a **sequel** to the one before it. Every year you build on what you learned the previous year. With these school changes also come life changes. As you grow older, you will be allowed to do more things. But you will also be responsible for more things. At first, each challenge might confuse you, but you will figure out how to conquer it **momentarily**.

You might notice a big difference when you go to middle school. Right now, you probably have the same classes all year. But in middle school, your classes might be in different **terms**. Some of your classes may change from one half of the year to the next. And, of course, your schoolwork will be more difficult, but also more interesting! High school will be another big change. You'll have lots of classes to keep track of. You may have a lot of things to do outside of school, too. It'll be a busy time!

Someday, you might go to college. You will **immediately** know that college is different, too. In fact, it will be different from every other **episode** of school you have been through. Right now, you cannot be **tardy** for your classes. You will get in trouble. In college, not all students are **punctual**. Students sometimes come to classes late. The teacher might tell them not to do that again. The teacher does not usually talk to their parents. In college, you alone will be responsible for getting to class and learning.

That freedom can be great. But it can also be difficult. Remember that each year of school prepares you for the next one. So learn all you can. Try your hardest. And before you know it, time will change you into a great adult!

Practice the Context Clues Strategy Here is one of the boldfaced words from the essay on page 128. Use the context clues strategy you learned in Part 1 on page 117 to figure out the meaning of this word.

momentarily

Read the sentence that uses the word *momentarily*. Read some of the sentences around the word.

Look for context clues. What words or ideas show you **What the Word Is Used For?**

_____

_____

Think about the context clues. What other helpful information do you know?

_____

_____

Predict a meaning for the word *momentarily*.

_____

_____

Check your Word Wisdom Dictionary to be sure of the meaning of the word *momentarily*. Write the definition here.

_____

_____

🔒 Unlock the Meanings

Phonetic Respellings Long words can be hard to say. The same is true of words that are said differently from the way they are spelled. A dictionary can show you how to say a word. After each word in a dictionary, you'll see the word respelled to help you say it. The letters and symbols show you how to say the word correctly. Stress marks tell which syllable to put force on when you say the word.

mo•men•tar•i•ly /mō′ mən **târ′** ə lē/

A heavy accent mark and boldface show which syllable is stressed the most.
A light accent mark shows which syllable is stressed a little.

Choose the Correct Pronunciation Read each word. After the word are two respellings. Circle the respelling that shows the correct way to say the word. Use a dictionary if you need help. You may also refer to the pronunciation key in your Word Wisdom Dictionary.

1 sequel   a. **sē′** kwəl   b. si **kwəl′**

2 tardy   a. **tär′** dē   b. **tär′** dē

3 frequent   a. **frĕ′** kwĭnt   b. **frĕ′** kwənt

4 punctual   a. pŭnk **shəl′**   b. **pŭngk′** chōō əl

5 tedious   a. **tē′** dē əs   b. **tē′** dōōs

6 routine   a. rə **tīn′**   b. rōō **tēn′**

7 term   a. tûrm   b. tĕrm

8 momentarily   a. mō′ mən **târ′** ə lē b. mŏ mən **tär′** ə lē

9 eventually   a. ē ven′ shə lē   b. ĭ **vĕn′** chōō ə lē

10 episode   a. **ĕp′** ĭ sōd   b. ēp ĭ söd

Find the Meaning

1. Use context clues.
2. Look for a familiar root, prefix, or suffix.
3. If the context or a word part doesn't help, check the dictionary.

Define the Words Follow the steps above to write the meaning of each boldfaced word. Write 1, 2, or 3 to show which steps you used.

WORD LIST

routine
eventually
frequent
sequel
momentarily
term
immediately
episode
tardy
punctual

1 Because I woke up late today, I was **tardy**.

_____

2 Please wait another minute. We'll be leaving **momentarily**.

_____

3 I read the **sequel** to the book to find out what happened next.

_____

4 The meeting must start at four o'clock. Please be **punctual**.

_____

5 The baby fell asleep **immediately** after dinner.

_____

6 This bus makes **frequent** stops to let people off and on.

_____

7 In the United States, the president's **term** of office is four years.

_____

8 The car crash was an upsetting **episode** in her life.

_____

9 After being held up by traffic, we **eventually** arrived.

_____

10 I brush my teeth as part of my morning **routine**.

_____

Process the Meanings

WORD LIST

- routine
- eventually
- frequent
- sequel
- momentarily
- term
- immediately
- episode
- tardy
- punctual

Check the Meanings   Write **C** if the boldfaced word is used correctly. Write **I** if it is used incorrectly.

1 My morning **routine** includes walking to the school bus stop every day. _____

2 The play will start two hours late. It will begin **momentarily**. _____

3 This is the first book in the series. It's the **sequel**. _____

4 When Jody heard the doorbell, she **immediately** ran to open the door. _____

5 Living in a tent for a month was an exciting **episode** in my life. _____

Identify Synonyms and Antonyms   Read each pair of words. Write **S** if the words are the same (synonyms). Write **O** if the words are opposites (antonyms). The boldfaced words are from the Word List.

6 **tardy**, early   _____

7 **eventually**, instantly   _____

8 **term**, period   _____

9 **punctual**, late   _____

10 **frequent**, often   _____

11 **routine**, same way   _____

12 **episode**, event   _____

Apply What You've Learned

Complete the Analogies Choose the word that best completes each statement. Write the word on the blank line.

1 Later is to future as **immediately** is to _____.
  a. now   b. tomorrow   c. yesterday

2 Few is to many as **frequent** is to _____.
  a. never   b. often   c. always

3 Introduction is to begin as **sequel** is to _____.
  a. start   b. continue   c. stop

4 Earth is to land area as **term** is to _____.
  a. short weekend   b. long year   c. time period

5 Sometime is to someday as **momentarily** is to _____.
  a. never   b. whenever   c. soon

Show Word Understanding Complete each sentence.

6 If you are **tardy** to soccer practice, you are _____

_____

7 A happy **episode** in my life was _____

_____

8 I will **eventually** _____

_____

9 It's important to be **punctual** when _____

_____

10 Part of my **routine** after school is _____

_____

Write It! What is your daily routine? Write about it using as many words from the Word List in Part 3 as you can.

Review

for Word Wisdom

WORD LIST

- prior
- news
- timely
- time frame
- indefinite
- tedious
- precaution
- schedule
- completion
- final
- renovate
- finalist
- definite
- novel
- infinite
- define
- contemporary
- renew
- temporary
- novelty
- routine
- eventually
- frequent
- sequel
- momentarily
- term
- immediately
- episode
- tardy
- punctual

Sort by Final Letters Look at each word in the Word List. Sort the words by the letter they end with. Write each word in the correct column. Then study each word. Look for the roots *fin* (end), *new, nov* (new), and *temp* (time). If a word has one of those roots, circle the word.

Words ending in y	Words ending in e	Words ending in other letters

Choose the Words That Don't Belong Read each group of vocabulary words. Only two words in each group have similar meanings. On the line, write the word that has a different meaning from the other two words.

1 timely, punctual, define   _____

2 renew, finalist, renovate   _____

3 novelty, final, completion   _____

4 term, news, time frame   _____

5 schedule, routine, sequel   _____

Show Word Knowledge Follow the directions. Write your answers on the lines.

6 Name something you need to be **punctual** for.

_____

_____

7 Explain what the word *infinite* means.

_____

8 List some things you do each day **prior** to going to school.

_____

_____

9 Tell about a **novel** idea you or someone else once had.

_____

10 Name something you should do **immediately** if you see a house on fire.

_____

_____

Taking Vocabulary Tests

Practice Test   Below are five short paragraphs. Each is followed by an incomplete sentence and four answer choices. Fill in the circle of the item that best completes the sentence.

1   My family belongs to a health club. To use the club, you have to be a member. Each year, we **renew** our membership.

The word **renew** means

○ find.   ○ end.
○ restart.   ○ enjoy.

2   I take the school bus home every day. Along the way, the bus makes **frequent** stops. It takes about twenty minutes for me to get home.

The word **frequent** means

○ one.   ○ hardly any.
○ many.   ○ few.

3   Every autumn, loads of leaves fall from the trees. They cover my backyard and front lawn. It's my job to rake up the huge pile. It's a **tedious** job.

The word **tedious** means

○ tiring and boring.   ○ fun and exciting.
○ difficult and cruel.   ○ cool and relaxing.

4   Yesterday, I went skateboarding. To avoid getting hurt, I wore a helmet and knee pads. I did this as a **precaution**.

The word **precaution** means

○ legal rule.   ○ smart idea.
○ first aid.   ○ safety measure.

5   My grandmother's favorite sweater is forty years old. For her birthday, we bought her a stylish, **contemporary** sweater. She loves her new sweater.

The word **contemporary** means

○ old.   ○ modern.
○ colorful.   ○ wool.

Play with Language

Solve the Puzzle Use the clues and vocabulary words in the box below to complete the crossword puzzle.

term	routine	tardy	momentarily
episode	definite	final	sequel
	news	temporary	

Down

1 a movie that continues the story from an earlier movie

2 soon

3 a set time period

4 late

8 recent information

Across

5 a separate event

6 a set way of doing things

7 last

9 for certain

10 lasting for only a short time

Speak It! Pretend that you are a "polite expert." Give a talk on ways in which people can be polite. Here is an example: "Don't remind people of embarrassing **episodes** they'd rather forget." Use as many words from this unit as you can.

Time Part 4 **137**

Context Clues

for Word Wisdom

Marc Brown:
The Writer Behind Arthur

Perhaps you've read an Arthur book or watched the *Arthur* television show. Arthur's creator, Marc Brown, is someone who loves being a writer. You can read more about him in the essay below.

Marc Brown is the **author** of the Arthur books. Brown also draws the pictures in the books. As a child, Brown told, wrote, and drew his own stories. He remembers how his Grandma Thora used to praise his artwork. She would save his drawings in her dresser drawer.

The character Arthur was born one night when Marc Brown was telling his own son a bedtime story. The story was about an aardvark named Arthur who hated his nose. That story became the first book in the Arthur **series**. Today there are more than twenty books in the collection.

Readers love the Arthur books because they are about real **issues**. The stories are about family life, school, and friendships. Brown's books **portray** some of the fears and problems that children have. At the same time, the stories are **humorous** and fun to read.

Sometimes, Brown's stories begin with a **brainstorm,** or a sudden idea. So that he never forgets a good idea, Brown keeps an idea drawer. At any time, he may **scribble** a good idea quickly onto a piece of paper and put it in his idea drawer. The idea may stay in the drawer for years before becoming a story.

Writing a book takes a lot of work. First, Brown writes the story. Then it's time to **edit** it by changing some things to make the story just right. After he draws the pictures, the story and drawings can be turned into a book.

Marc Brown visits schools around the country. If you ever meet him, you might ask him for his **autograph**. You might even ask him to write his autograph in an Arthur book if you own one.

When students ask him about becoming a writer, Marc Brown has good **advice**. He tells them to read a lot, keep a journal, and write about whatever interests them. He also tells students that to get good at writing, they have to practice, practice, and practice some more.

Context Clues Strategy

Look for How Something Is Done

EXAMPLE: In my book report, I *mentioned* the author by writing a few details about her.

CLUE: The words *by writing a few details* tell how *mentioned* was done.

Here is one strategy for using context clues to understand the word *edit* from the essay about Marc Brown.

Read the sentence with the unknown word. Read a sentence or two around it.

First, Brown writes the story. Then it's time to edit it by changing some things to make the story just right.

Look for context clues. What clues showing **How Something Is Done** can you find?

The phrase *by changing some things to make the story just right* is a clue to how *editing* is done.

Think about the context clues and other information you may already know.

I know that good writers read their writing and fix it.

Predict a meaning for the word.

The word *edit* must mean "to fix and make better."

Check the Word Wisdom Dictionary to be sure of the meaning.

Edit means "to correct written material."

Practice the Strategy Here is one of the boldfaced words from the essay on page 138. Use the context clues strategy on page 139 to figure out the meaning of the word.

scribble

Read the sentence that uses the word *scribble*. Read some of the sentences around the word.

Look for context clues. What clues showing **How Something Is Done** can you find?

_____

_____

_____

Think about the context clues. What other helpful information do you know?

_____

_____

_____

Predict a meaning for the word *scribble*.

_____

_____

_____

Check your Word Wisdom Dictionary to be sure of the meaning of the word *scribble*. Write the definition here.

_____

_____

_____

WORD LIST

author
series
issue
portray
humorous
brainstorm
✔ scribble
✔ edit
autograph
advice

Use Context Clues The two vocabulary words that you have learned so far are checked off in the Word List. In the first column, write the other eight words from the Word List. In the second column, predict a meaning for each word. Then look up the meaning in your Word Wisdom Dictionary. In the third column, write the dictionary meaning that fits the context.

Vocabulary Word	Your Prediction	Dictionary Says
1		
2		
3		
4		
5		
6		
7		
8		

Process the Meanings

WORD LIST

author

series

issue

portray

humorous

brainstorm

scribble

edit

autograph

advice

Complete the Groups Choose the word from the Word List that best completes each group. The correct word will have a similar meaning to the other words in the group. Write the word on the line.

1 funny, amusing, _____

2 help, suggestion, _____

3 correct, fix, _____

4 group, collection, _____

5 topic, problem, _____

Choose the Correct Word Write a word from the Word List to complete each sentence. You will have to add an ending to two words. Do not repeat any words that you wrote as answers above.

6 I just thought of a great idea. Listen to my

_____

7 The _____ of this book is a very

fine writer.

8 I was in a big rush to finish the spelling test, so I

_____ the last answer.

9 In this great story, the boy who saved the man is

_____ as a hero.

10 The famous baseball player from my town wrote his

_____ on my baseball.

Review the Meanings Decide if each sentence is true or false. Write **T** for true or **F** for false on the line.

_____ **1** A **humorous** person would make people laugh.

_____ **2** An author would **edit** a book after it is in the bookstore.

_____ **3** You might **scribble** someone's telephone number when you are in a rush.

_____ **4** The **author** of a book usually writes the story.

_____ **5** An **autograph** is the story of a famous person's life.

_____ **6** A **brainstorm** is an old idea.

Answer the Questions Answer each question by writing a complete sentence.

7 How is the wolf **portrayed** in the story _The Three Little Pigs_?

_____

8 What **advice** would you give to someone who always forgets her homework?

_____

9 What is a book **series** that you have read or heard about?

_____

10 What **issues** might be discussed in a book about health?

_____

Write It! Write five sentences that use two words from the Part 1 Word List in each sentence. Here is an example: The doctor has good **advice** about this health **issue**.

PART 2

Latin and Greek Roots

for Word Wisdom

Reporting the News:

What Is a Journalist?

Do you watch the news on television? The people who share the news are called *journalists.* **Some journalists are also called** *reporters.* **Their job is to collect the news and report it to us. But journalists do much more than that.**

You learn many things from the news. You find out about things going on in your own town. You learn about things going on in the world. You learn about sports and the weather. There is a lot of **data** to share each day.

You can find journalists in many different places. They appear on television or write for newspapers or magazines. Journalists work in big cities and in small towns. They travel to faraway countries. Journalists are all over the world!

Proper **grammar** is important to journalists. They share the news in a way that makes it easy to understand. They **describe** facts and ideas clearly. They might even use charts and **diagrams** in their work. Good communication is very important. Sometimes television

reporters read from a **script**. Other times they don't have anything to read—they speak from their minds. But reporters always try to share what is important.

There are **editorials** in newspapers, magazines, and on TV news shows. In this kind of news report, a person shares his or her opinions about a subject. Some people may agree. Others may disagree. The report might be only a **paragraph**. Each **edition** is different. But it will always make you think.

Some people buy **subscriptions** to newspapers and magazines. They might do this because they trust that source, or because they like one writer a lot. Some journalists are famous. They appear on our televisions or in our newspapers every day. Some even write books. Fans may ask them to **inscribe** a message in their books.

A lot goes on in the world each day. Journalists make sure that we keep up with the news. They help us learn. And, sometimes, they entertain us. Is this a job that you might enjoy someday?

Practice the Context Clues Strategy Here is one of the boldfaced words from the essay on page 144. Use the context clues strategy you learned in Part 1 on page 139 to figure out the meaning of this word.

describe

Read the sentence that uses the word *describe*. Read some of the sentences around the word.

Look for context clues to the word's meaning. Can you find clues that show **How Something Is Done**?

_____

_____

_____

Think about the context clues. What other helpful information do you know?

_____

_____

_____

Predict a meaning for the word *describe*.

_____

_____

_____

Check your Word Wisdom Dictionary to be sure of the meaning of the word *describe*. Write the definition here.

_____

_____

_____

🔒 Unlock the Meanings

Many English words come from Latin or Greek roots. If you know the meaning of different roots, you can often unlock the meaning of new words. Some words you learned in Part 1 have a Latin or a Greek root. Each root is related to language and writing.

Latin Root: **dit, dat**	Greek Root: **graph, gram**	Latin Root: **scrib, script**
meaning: to give	meaning: to write	meaning: to write
English word: *edit*	English word: *autograph*	English word: *scribble*
meaning: to correct writing	meaning: a person's handwritten signature	meaning: to write quickly or carelessly

WORD LIST

- data
- grammar
- describe
- diagram
- script
- editorial
- paragraph
- edition
- subscription
- inscribe

Sort by Roots   Sort the words in the Word List by their roots. Write each word under the correct root. Then think of other words you know that come from the same Latin and Greek roots. Write each word under the correct root.

Latin Root: dit, dat	Greek Root: graph, gram	Latin Root: scrib, script

Language and Writing

Prefix	Meaning
para-	beside
sub-	under

Example

para- (beside) + **graph** (write) = **paragraph**

Use Roots and Prefixes Circle the root and any prefix you find in the boldfaced words below. Use context clues, roots, and prefixes to write the meaning of each word. Check your definitions in the Word Wisdom Dictionary.

1 We use the rules of **grammar** to speak and write correctly.

_____

2 To learn my lines in the play, I memorized the **script**.

_____

3 A computer can store a lot of **data**.

_____

4 This **diagram** shows how the pieces go together.

_____

5 Grandma **inscribed** the book she gave to me.

_____

6 I wrote an answer to the question in a short **paragraph**.

_____

7 Zack's uncle gave him a magazine **subscription** for his birthday.

_____

8 The newest **edition** of this dictionary has one hundred extra words in it.

_____

9 My mother saw a coat I might like. I asked her to **describe** it to me.

_____

10 The writer of this **editorial** has strong opinions about recycling.

Process the Meanings

WORD LIST

WORD LIST

data

grammar

describe

diagram

script

editorial

paragraph

edition

subscription

inscribe

Identify Similar Words Circle the word that has the MOST similar meaning to each boldfaced word.

1 Please **describe** what you saw.
   a. scream   b. explain   c. hear

2 Do you understand the **data**?
   a. information   b. poster   c. story

3 Look at the **diagram**.
   a. drawing   b. book   c. dictionary

4 This is the newest **edition**.
   a. place   b. version   c. paper

5 Let's read the **script**.
   a. magazine   b. exercises   c. play

Use the Words Correctly in Writing Rewrite each sentence in your own words. Include the word in parentheses in your sentence. You will need to add an ending to one word.

6 Writing incomplete sentences goes against the rules of writing correctly. (grammar)

_____

7 The author of this article wants lower prices. (editorial)

_____

8 I would like to receive this monthly magazine. (subscription)

_____

9 We had to write a few sentences about food. (paragraph)

_____

10 Look at this message written on the stone. (inscribe)

_____

Solve the Riddles Write the best word from the Word List for each clue.

_____ **1** I am rules about how to speak and write.

_____ **2** Do this to carve a message.

_____ **3** If the actors know me well, the audience may clap a lot.

_____ **4** I'll do this to tell you all about it.

_____ **5** If you have me, your newspaper will be delivered to you.

Demonstrate Word Knowledge Choose the best word from the Word List to complete each sentence.

6 It's **not** a simple drawing, but a complex _____

7 It's **not** an old version, but a new _____

8 It's **not** just one fact, but a large amount of _____

9 It's **not** a news article with facts only, but an _____

10 It's **not** a whole page of writing, but one short _____

11 It's **not** a book, but a funny movie _____

12 It's **not** slang, but good _____

13 It's **not** a a free issue, but a monthly magazine _____

14 It's **not** "to erase a message," but "to _____" one.

15 It's **not** "to confuse," but "to clearly _____"

Speak It! Find a newspaper and look through it. Describe what you see. Use several Part 2 words.

PART 3 Reference Skills

for Word Wisdom

A Writer for All Ages:
Shel Silverstein

Have you ever read something written by Shel Silverstein? As you might know, he wrote many stories and poems. Children and adults around the world enjoy his writing.

Shel Silverstein's writing is so popular that there are many **translations** of his books. In fact, we can read his books in thirty different languages! You can read a Shel Silverstein book in any part of the world, but the author had a hard time getting his early books **printed**. One of these books was *The Giving Tree*. People said it was too sad. It is the story about a tree that loved a boy. This simple **summary** might sound silly, but the book isn't. Of course, Silverstein did finally get this story made into a book. And millions of people have read it. Many adults love this book as much as children do!

Another popular book by Silverstein is *Lafcadio, The Lion Who Shot Back*. It is the story of a lion that learns self-defense. The book is divided into **chapters,** and it includes many of Silverstein's own drawings. In fact, he drew a lot of pictures to go with his writing.

Silverstein also liked to write **poems**. His book *Where the Sidewalk Ends* has many poems. The book *A Light in the Attic* does, too. Poems are the **text** of the books. Many of Silverstein's poems are very silly, but his books are fun not just because of the words. His drawings are in these books, too! Most of his drawings do not have **captions** with them. That's because the pictures often illustrate the **verses** of the poems. Or maybe the poems tell about the drawings—it could go either way!

Some of Silverstein's poems are made up of many **stanzas**. Other poems have just a few. But most of them will make you smile. And almost all of them will make you think.

Silverstein passed away in 1999. Many people were very sad. People all over the world wrote **articles** about him. They told him good-bye. They said that they would miss him. But we will always have his writing and his drawings. And both children and adults will enjoy his great works for years to come.

Practice the Context Clues Strategy Here is one of the boldfaced words from the essay on page 150. Use the context clues strategy you learned in Part 1 on page 139 to figure out the meaning of this word.

translations

Read the sentence that uses the word *translations*. Read some of the sentences around the word.

Look for context clues to the word's meaning. Can you find any clues that tell **How Something Is Done?**

_____

_____

_____

Think about the context clues. What other helpful information do you know?

_____

_____

Predict a meaning for the word *translations*.

_____

_____

_____

Check your Word Wisdom Dictionary to be sure of the meaning of the word *translation*. Write the definition here.

_____

_____

_____

Unlock the Meanings

Model Sentences In a dictionary, model sentences often appear after the definition of a word. They are helpful because they show you how the word is used in a sentence. Here is a dictionary entry with a sample sentence.

sum•ma•ry /sŭm′ ə rē/ n. a short statement that gives the main idea about something. *Mary read the story and wrote a summary about it.*

↑model sentence

Match the Model Sentences Below are five different definitions followed by five model sentences for the word *print*. Match each definition with the correct model sentence. Write the letter of the definition on the line.

Definitions

a. **print** /prĭnt/ *v.* to produce words on a page with a machine that uses ink.

b. **print** /prĭnt/ *v.* to write without joining the letters.

c. **print** /prĭnt/ *v.* to publish.

d. **print** /prĭnt/ *n.* a mark made in or on a surface using pressure.

e. **print** /prĭnt/ *n.* a specific pattern on a material or fabric.

Model Sentences

_____ **1** My teacher asks us to **print** our name on our papers.

_____ **2** I like the shirt with the colorful **print**.

_____ **3** After I finish writing this letter on the computer, I will **print** it.

_____ **4** Look at the **print** of my foot in the sand.

_____ **5** This magazine **prints** poems that third graders write.

Find the Meaning
1. Use context clues.
2. Look for a familiar root, prefix, or suffix.
3. If the context or a word part doesn't help, check the dictionary.

Define the Words Follow the steps above to write the meaning of each boldfaced word. Then write 1, 2, or 3 to show which steps you used.

WORD LIST
- translation
- print
- summary
- chapter
- poem
- text
- caption
- verse
- stanza
- article

1 Let's sing the first **verse** of the song together.

_____

2 I have one more **chapter** to read in this book.

_____

3 The class read an English **translation** of the Spanish story.

_____

4 Can you give me a **summary** of the short story you read?

_____

5 After I looked at the pictures in the book, I read the **text**.

_____

6 The **caption** below this photograph tells where it was taken.

_____

7 This magazine is full of interesting **articles** to read.

_____

8 I wrote a **poem** that rhymes.

_____

9 The newspaper **printed** a story about the snowstorm.

_____

10 This is a short poem. It has only two **stanzas**.

_____

Process the Meanings

WORD LIST

WORD LIST

translation

print

summary

chapter

poem

text

caption

verse

stanza

article

Choose the Correct Word Write the word from the Word List that best completes each sentence.

1 Before I learned English, I needed a very clear

_____ of everything I heard or read.

2 Below the photo is a _____ that tells

who took the picture.

3 "My Shadow," by the poet Robert Louis Stevenson, is my

favorite _____.

4 The newspaper will _____ the story.

5 This long poem has twelve _____!

Replace the Underlined Words Write the best word from the Word List to take the place of the underlined word or words in each sentence.

6 Rob can give you a <u>statement that tells the main ideas</u> of

the book he just read. _____

7 My favorite dictionary has pictures as well as <u>words on the

page</u>. _____

8 Do you know the first <u>few lines</u> of "America the Beautiful"

by heart? _____

9 The crime is solved in the book's last <u>section</u>. _____

_____

10 There is a funny <u>piece of writing</u> about dogs in this

magazine. _____

Apply What You've Learned

Show Word Knowledge   Answer the questions.

1 What might your teacher ask you to write a **summary** of? _____

_____

2 What is a **verse** from a song that you know? _____

_____

_____

3 What makes a **poem** different from a story? _____

_____

4 When would you need a **translation** of a book? _____

_____

5 What does a newspaper **print**? _____

_____

Demonstrate Understanding   Draw a line under the correct ending for each sentence.

6 You would read a **chapter** in a _____.
dictionary   book   newspaper

7 In a textbook, you would find a **caption** under a _____.
picture   page number   title

8 You would read an **article** in a _____.
cartoon   poem   magazine

9 You would find a **stanza** in a _____.
test   newspaper   poem

10 The **text** of a book is its _____.
pictures   story   writer

Write It! Write about your favorite things to read. Use as many words from the Part 3 Word List as you can.

PART 4

Review

for Word Wisdom

WORD LIST

author
series
issue
portray
humorous
brainstorm
scribble
edit
autograph
advice
data
grammar
describe
diagram
script
editorial
paragraph
edition
subscription
inscribe
translation
print
summary
chapter
poem
text
caption
verse
stanza
article

Sort by Categories   Read the name of each group below. Think about each word in the Word List. Sort the words into the groups. (One word fits in more than one group.) Be ready to explain your choices. Then study each word. Look for the roots *dit, dat* (give), *graph, gram* (write), and *scrib, script* (write). If a word has one of those roots, circle the word.

Writing that you read	Things you do related to writing	Other words

Choose the Correct Word Circle the vocabulary word that correctly completes each sentence.

1 A poem is divided into (stanzas, chapters).

2 The (translation, caption) next to the photo tells more about it.

3 I wrote a (subscription, summary) of the book for my book report.

4 My teacher gives me good (advice, issues) when I have a problem.

5 The magazine is delivered to me because I have a (translation, subscription).

Show Word Knowledge Write **yes** or **no** to answer each question. Then explain your answer to show your understanding of the boldfaced vocabulary words.

6 When you **edit** your writing, should you check your **grammar**? Why?

_____

7 If a **text** is written in your language, would you want a **translation**? Why?

_____

8 Would you want the **autograph** of an **author** who writes a best-selling **series**? Why?

_____

9 In a textbook **chapter** about pollution, will most of the **paragraphs** be about the main **issue**? Why?

_____

10 If you want to know the news, would you read **articles** from last week's **edition** of the paper? Why?

_____

Taking Vocabulary Tests

Some tests ask you to find a word that has the same meaning as a word that is underlined in a phrase. Think about the meaning of the underlined word. Some of the answer choices may make sense in the phrase, but they don't have the same meaning as the underlined word. If you are stuck or you can't decide between two answers, skip the question. Go back to it later.

Sample:

inscribe a message
- ○ tell
- ○ hear
- ○ give
- ◉ write

Practice Test Fill in the circle for the word or words that have the SAME or ALMOST THE SAME meaning as the underlined word.

1 scribble your name
- ○ spell carefully
- ○ erase completely
- ○ say slowly
- ○ write quickly

2 finish the chapter
- ○ section
- ○ poster
- ○ mail
- ○ title

3 a famous author
- ○ actor
- ○ writer
- ○ illustrator
- ○ singer

4 read the script
- ○ play
- ○ paper
- ○ advertisement
- ○ ticket

5 interesting data
- ○ people
- ○ facts
- ○ places
- ○ time

6 a humorous story
- ○ boring
- ○ sad
- ○ funny
- ○ long

7 a clear diagram
- ○ drawing
- ○ photograph
- ○ dictionary
- ○ word

8 have a brainstorm
- ○ big problem
- ○ sudden idea
- ○ funny joke
- ○ long book

9 article in a magazine
- ○ crossword puzzle
- ○ photographs and maps
- ○ advertisement
- ○ piece of writing

10 first verse
- ○ part of a short story
- ○ lines in a poem
- ○ front-page news story
- ○ part of a book

Build New Words

Add Suffixes A suffix is a word ending. The suffix *-able* means "able to be." Make new words by adding and subtracting letters if needed, and by adding suffixes. Here is an example.

Word	+ or -	+ Suffix	= New Word
define	– e	+ -able	= definable

Add or subtract letters as shown. Then add the suffix *-able* to change each vocabulary word into a new word.

Word	+ or -	+ Suffix	= New Word
print		+ -able	
portray		+ -able	
describe	– e	+ -able	
diagram	+ m	+ -able	
advice	– ce + s	+ -able	

Speak It! Interview a classmate about one of his or her favorite books. Use as many words from this unit as you can. Here is a sample question: "Does the book have any **humorous** characters?"

Context Clues

for Word Wisdom

The Unsinkable Ship That Sank:
The Titanic

On April 10, 1912, the *Titanic* set sail from England to New York. People were excited to be on this amazing ship. No one knew that this would be the ship's first and only voyage.

In 1912, near the beginning of the twentieth **century,** the *Titanic* was the largest ship in the world. The mighty *Titanic* was **immense,** like a huge floating hotel. It was as long as three football fields. It was taller than a ten-story building.

People believed that the ship was unsinkable. The body of the ship had sixteen compartments. Even if water flooded four of the sixteen compartments, the ship would still float.

While at sea, the *Titanic* was warned by other ships about huge icebergs. At night, those icebergs were hard to see.

On April 14, at a little before midnight, the side of the *Titanic* hit an iceberg. Sharp pieces of ice scraped the ship and tore holes into it. Water rushed into the compartments. **Fragments** from the huge iceberg fell onto the deck of the ship.

The captain needed to **assess** the situation. He learned that there was a large **amount** of damage. Five compartments were filled with water. The *Titanic* would probably sink in less than two hours.

The *Titanic* called for help. Another ship heard the call, but it would take hours for it to arrive. By then, it would be too late. The *Titanic* had a terrible **shortage** of lifeboats. There were life jackets, but the water was freezing. More than 2,000 people were on board. Only 705 people survived.

After the disaster, **numerous** laws were made to prevent such a tragedy from happening again, or at least **minimize** the damage. Every ship now must have enough lifeboats for the number of people on board. Ships must also hold lifeboat drills.

In 1985, a team of scientists discovered the shipwreck. The *Titanic* was found on the ocean floor at a **depth** of 13,000 feet, or 4,000 **meters**. (A meter is about as long as a baseball bat.) The *Titanic* is still on the ocean floor today.

UNIT

8

Measurement

Context Clues Strategy

Look for What the Word Is Like

EXAMPLE: Like a ruler, a *yardstick* can be used to measure the length of something.

CLUE: The words *like a ruler* compare a *yardstick* with something you already know.

Here is another strategy for using context clues to understand new words. Use the strategy to learn the word *meter* from the essay on page 160.

Read the sentence with the unknown word. Read a sentence or two around it.

The Titanic *was found on the ocean floor at a **depth** of 13,000 feet, or 4,000 **meters**. (A meter is about as long as a baseball bat.)*

Look for context clues. What clues showing **What the Word Is Like** can you find?

The words *about as long as a baseball bat* are a clue about what a *meter* is like.

Think about the context clues and other information you may already know.

The sentence says that 4,000 meters is also 13,000 feet. I know that a meter must be a kind of measurement.

Predict a meaning for the word.

The word *meter* must mean a measure of length.

Check your Word Wisdom Dictionary to be sure of the meaning.

Meter means "a unit of length in the metric system equal to 39.37 inches."

Practice the Strategy The boldfaced word below is from the *Titanic* article on page 160. Use the context clues strategy on page 161 to figure out the meaning of the word.

immense

📖 **Read** the sentence that uses the word *immense*. Read some of the sentences around the word.

🔍 **Look** for context clues. What clues showing **What the Word Is Like** can you find?

_____

_____

💡 **Think** about the context clues. What other helpful information do you know?

_____

_____

➡ **Predict** a meaning for the word *immense*.

_____

_____

✔ **Check** the Word Wisdom Dictionary to be sure of the meaning of the word *immense*. Write the definition here.

_____

_____

Use Context Clues Two words you have learned from the article are checked off in the Word List. In the first column, write the other eight words from the Word List. In the second column, use context clues to predict a meaning for each word. Then look up the meanings in the Word Wisdom Dictionary. In the third column, write the definition that fits the context.

WORD LIST

century
✔ immense
fragment
assess
amount
shortage
numerous
minimize
depth
✔ meter

Vocabulary Word	Your Prediction	Dictionary Says
1		
2		
3		
4		
5		
6		
7		
8		

Process the Meanings

WORD LIST

- century
- immense
- fragment
- assess
- amount
- shortage
- numerous
- minimize
- depth
- meter

Find the Opposites Read each sentence. Write the word from the Word List that has the opposite meaning of the boldfaced word or words.

1 The opposite of **tiny** is _____.

2 The opposite of **few** is _____.

3 The opposite of to **make as large as possible** is to

_____.

4 The opposite of having **extra** is having a

_____.

5 The opposite of a **whole** is a _____.

Replace the Words Replace the boldfaced word or words in each sentence with a word from the Word List. Write the word on the line.

6 What is the **sum** of the damage here?

_____

7 This test will **judge** your math skills.

_____

8 The **deepness** of the diving pool is twenty feet.

_____

9 This pole is a **little more than three feet** long.

_____

10 In the past **one hundred years**, there have been many

inventions. _____

Apply What You've Learned

Complete the sentences Finish each sentence.

1 In a desert, there is usually a **shortage** of _____

2 It is my teacher's job to **assess** _____

3 If I want to dive into a pool, I must first make sure the **depth** is

_____

4 If a large **amount** of rain falls, _____

5 When I take a test, I want to **minimize** _____

_____

Find Examples Each word is followed by two examples. Only one is an example of the word. Write **E** next to the correct example.

6 meter   _____ about as long as a thumbnail

               _____ about as long as a baseball bat

7 immense   _____ a mouse

               _____ an elephant

8 fragment   _____ a piece of glass from a broken vase

               _____ a cookie that fell on the floor

9 century   _____ the years between 1800 and 1900

               _____ the years between 2000 and 2005

10 numerous   _____ a bird resting on a telephone wire

               _____ a flock of birds on a telephone wire

Write It! Write three sentences that begin "I wish...." Use a vocabulary word from Part 1 in each sentence.

PART 2

Latin and Greek Roots

for Word Wisdom

How the World Measures:
The Metric System

Most countries use the same system of measurement. This system is built around just one unit—the meter.

In 1995, France celebrated a special birthday. It was the **bicentennial** of the **metric** system. Two hundred years before, France was the first country to use the metric system. Now ninety-five **percent** of the world uses this system of measurement.

The United States is one of the few countries that does not use the metric system. Well, we do not *totally* use it. But you can find many examples of it. In nature there are insects with metric names. The **centipede** is one. The prefix *centi-* comes from the metric system. It means "hundred."

In math, most students learn **geometry**. This study is based on the metric system. You can see the word part *metr* in that word. Do you know what the **diameter** of a circle is? Again, you see the word *meter*. This word is also taken from the metric system.

Look at the **speedometer** in a car. It tells you how many miles your car travels in an hour. But it also shows kilometers per hour. *Kilometer* is a way to measure distance using the metric system.

In this country, we use Fahrenheit to measure temperature. We would say, "It's 68 degrees Fahrenheit outside." But the metric system uses *Celsius* to measure temperature. You might need to change the temperature from Fahrenheit to Celsius. Subtract 32 from the Fahrenheit temperature and divide that number by 1.8. So, 68 **minus** 32 is 36, and 36 divided by 1.8 is 20. The temperature 68 degrees Fahrenheit is the same as 20 degrees Celsius.

There are charts to help you change numbers to the metric system. Large charts list many measurements. **Miniature** charts, which are much smaller, include only a few measurements. A "kitchen" chart tells what teaspoons are in the metric system. It gives you a **minimum** of information.

Try to learn the metric system. Someday our country might use it even more. After all, the rest of the world already does.

Practice the Context Clues Strategy Here is one of the boldfaced words from the essay on page 166. Use the context clues strategy you learned in Part 1 on page 161 to figure out the meaning of this word.

miniature

Read the sentence that uses the word *miniature*. Read some of the sentences around the word.

Look for context clues to the word's meaning. Can you find any words that tell **What the Word Is Like?**

_____

_____

_____

Think about the context clues. What other helpful information do you know?

_____

_____

_____

Predict a meaning for the word *miniature*.

_____

_____

_____

Check your Word Wisdom Dictionary to be sure of the meaning of the word *miniature*. Write the definition here.

_____

_____

_____

🔒 Unlock the Meanings

Many English words come from Latin and Greek roots. If you know the meaning of different roots, you can often unlock the meaning of new words. Some words you learned in Part 1 have a Latin or a Greek root. Each root is related to measurement.

Greek Root: **meter, metr**	Latin Root: **cent**	Latin Root: **min**
meaning: measure	meaning: hundred	meaning: small
English word: *meter*	English word: *century*	English word: *minimize*
meaning: a unit of measurement equal to 39.37 inches	meaning: a period of one hundred years	meaning: to make something as small as possible

WORD LIST

- bicentennial
- metric
- percent
- centipede
- geometry
- diameter
- speedometer
- minus
- miniature
- minimum

Sort by Roots Sort the words in the Word List by their roots. Write each word under the correct root. Then think of other words you know that come from the same Latin and Greek roots. Write each word in the correct place.

Greek Root: **meter, metr**	Latin Root: **cent**	Latin Root: **min**
_____	_____	_____
_____	_____	_____
_____	_____	_____
_____	_____	_____
_____	_____	_____
_____	_____	_____

Measurement

Prefix	Meaning
dia-	through
bi-	twice

Example

dia- (through) + **meter** (measure) = **diameter**

Use Roots and Prefixes Circle the root and any prefix you find in the boldfaced words below. Use context clues, roots, and prefixes to write the meaning of each word.

1 That bug with many legs must be a **centipede**.

_____

2 A subtraction problem always has a **minus** sign.

_____

3 The **miniature** furniture in the dollhouse is cute.

_____

4 The cup is fifty **percent**, or half, full.

_____

5 The **speedometer** shows that you are going very fast.

_____

6 We can't form a team unless there is a **minimum** of five players.

_____

7 If you like to learn about lines and shapes, you will enjoy **geometry**.

_____

8 Our country celebrated its **bicentennial** 200 years after it was born.

_____

9 Many countries use a **metric** system of measurement.

_____

10 To figure out how wide a circle is, measure its **diameter**.

_____

WORD LIST

- bicentennial
- metric
- percent
- centipede
- geometry
- diameter
- speedometer
- minus
- miniature
- minimum

Choose the Correct Words Write the vocabulary word that best completes each sentence.

1 If you study _____, you'll learn about shapes and angles.

2 We are traveling at sixty miles an hour, according to the _____.

3 A dime has a smaller _____ than a quarter has.

4 The school's spelling bee champion spelled one hundred _____ of the words correctly.

5 A centimeter is a unit of measurement in the _____ system.

6 The United States became a country in 1776. In 1976, it celebrated its _____.

7 Fifteen _____ seven equals eight.

8 The plane won't fly with so few passengers. There must be a _____ number of people on board.

9 This _____ shoe would probably fit on a baby doll.

10 How many legs does a _____ really have?

Solve the Riddles Write the best word from the Word List for each clue.

_____ **1** I stretch through the middle of a circle.

_____ **2** I come along every two hundred years.

_____ **3** You won't know how fast you're traveling

without me.

_____ **4** I'm written after the score on your test.

_____ **5** I'm also known as "take away."

_____ **6** Meters and grams are part of my system.

Complete the Analogies Choose the word that best completes each statement. Write the word on the line.

7 Enormous is to big as **miniature** is to _____.

  a. large   b. medium   c. small

8 Biology is to science as **geometry** is to _____.

  a. writing   b. math   c. history

9 Octopus is to arms as **centipede** is to _____.

  a. head   b. legs   c. ears

10 Most is to greatest as **minimum** is to _____.

  a. least   b. big   c. youngest

Speak It! Read the Word List aloud. After you say each word, say the first word that comes to mind. Write down the word you said. Compare your words with a partner.

PART 3

Reference Skills

for Word Wisdom

Surf's Up:

Measuring Up the Web

Sometimes it is fun to surf the Web. Other times, it's hard to find what you need. But there are many ways to successfully search the World Wide Web.

You can use the Internet to find information on nearly anything. You just need permission from an adult and knowledge of how to use a search engine. Search engines help you find information on the World Wide Web.

First, you have to know what you want to find. Maybe you want to learn about snowboarding. What happens if you type in the word *snow*? You'll have an **incomplete** search. You have to give the search engine more information.

Most searches you make will give you **multiple** choices. Often the **total** number of choices is too big. If you typed *snowboarding,* lots of choices would come up. It would take you a long time to look at two million Web pages! Some of these pages might be **identical** or, at least, almost the same.

The word *snowboarding* might be too general. Add other words to narrow your search. For example,

type *girl snowboarding*. You will have a **medium** number of choices. But there would still be too many pages to sort. It would be better if you had only a **fraction** of that amount.

You can narrow your search even more. Maybe you want to learn about girls in the history of snowboarding. Type the words *snowboarding girl history*. Or choose a certain **decade** as your focus. Type *snowboarding girl 1990s*. This is a good search. It has more details about what you're looking for. You can **double** your chances of finding useful Web pages.

Once you find a good Web page, there might be a lot of links to other snowboarding pages. You might see the same Web pages over and over. They can lead you in a **circular** path, around and around, back to where you started.

The Internet is a great place to learn. You can learn about topics like **diagonal** lines for math. You can learn about similes for English. You can learn about topics like sunspots and cells for science. The information is out there—you just need to find it! Once you find it, think about how the information "measures up."

Practice the Context Clues Strategy Here is one of the boldfaced words from the essay on page 172. Use the context clues strategy you learned in Part 1 on page 161 to figure out the meaning of this word.

identical

Read the sentence that uses the word *identical*. Read some of the sentences around the word.

Look for context clues to the word's meaning. Can you find any words that tell **What the Word Is Like**?

_____

_____

_____

Think about the context clues. What other helpful information do you know?

_____

_____

_____

Predict a meaning for the word *identical*.

_____

_____

_____

Check your Word Wisdom Dictionary to be sure of the meaning of the word *identical*. Write the definition here.

_____

_____

_____

The Thesaurus A thesaurus is a book of words and their synonyms. Synonyms are words that mean almost the same thing. Synonyms can add variety and new words to your writing and speaking. Look for a word in a thesaurus the same way you would look for a word in a dictionary.

Let's say you're trying to describe a *big* mountain and would like to find another word for *big*. Here are some synonyms that a thesaurus might list for the word *big*.

big: large, huge, enormous, great, vast, immense

Choose the Synonyms Read each boldfaced word and its synonyms. Then write the synonym that best replaces the boldfaced word in each sentence.

1 **identical:** matching, alike, equal
Five minus one is **identical** to four. _____

2 **small:** short, little, miniature, unimportant
Don't worry about **small** matters. _____

3 **hot:** warm, boiling, sizzling, burning
The bubbling water in the pot is **hot!** _____

4 **medium:** average, middle, halfway
Some girls and boys in my class are taller
than I am. I am not tall or short.
My height is **medium**. _____

5 **measure:** grade, weigh, mark off
We will **measure** the fruit on a scale. _____

1. Use context clues.
2. Look for a familiar root, prefix, or suffix.
3. If the context or a word part doesn't help, check the dictionary.

Define the Words Follow the three steps above to write the meaning of each boldfaced word. Then write 1, 2, or 3 to show which steps you used.

WORD LIST
incomplete
multiple
total
identical
medium
fraction
decade
double
circular
diagonal

1 After Tom fell off his bike, he had **multiple** bruises.

_____

2 I drew a **diagonal** line from opposite corners of the square.

_____

3 Amy just turned ten years old. She celebrated a **decade** of life.

_____

4 The twins look exactly alike. They are **identical**.

_____

5 I can eat only a **fraction** of the piece of pie.

_____

6 This fancy watch is **double** the price of the cheaper one.

_____

7 What is the **total** number of people coming to the party?

_____

8 The puzzle is **incomplete**. We must put in these final pieces.

_____

9 This large shirt is too big for me. The **medium** shirt fits perfectly.

_____

10 The toy train kept going around the **circular** track.

_____

Process the Meanings

WORD LIST

incomplete
multiple
total
identical
medium
fraction
decade
double
circular
diagonal

Match the Definitions Write the word from the Word List that matches each definition.

Definition	**Vocabulary Word**
1 average or middle	_____
2 round	_____
3 twice the amount	_____
4 a period of ten years	_____
5 slanting	_____

Use the Words Correctly in Writing Rewrite each sentence in your own words. Use the vocabulary word in parentheses in your sentence.

6 Do you mind if I wear the same coat as you? (identical)

_____

7 A small number of the marbles in the kit are chipped. (fraction)

_____

8 We must do all ten math problems for homework. (total)

_____

9 My test is not finished because I ran out of time. (incomplete)

_____

10 There are many answers to this question. (multiple)

_____

Apply What You've Learned

Show Word Knowledge Follow the directions.

1 Name some objects that are **circular** in shape.

_____

2 Name something that you wish you could have **double** of.

_____

3 Tell how many years are in a **decade**.

_____

4 Name two things in your classroom that are **identical**.

_____

5 Explain what it means for something to be **incomplete**.

_____

Answer the Questions Use what you have learned about each boldfaced vocabulary word to answer each question. Write **yes** or **no**.

6 If you draw a **diagonal** line, is the line slanted? _____

7 If a quiz is very easy, would you say it is **medium** hard? _____

8 If a book has eight chapters, does it have **multiple** chapters?

_____

9 If some classmates are home because they are sick, is a **fraction**

of the class absent? _____

10 Is the **total** price the full price you must pay? _____

Write It! Describe your home. Think about the inside and the outside of it. Use as many words from the Word List in Part 3 as you can.

PART 4

Review

for Word Wisdom

Sort by Categories Look at each word in the Word List. Sort the words into the groups below. The number in each box tells you how many words go with that group. Some words fit in more than one group.

WORD LIST

- century
- immense
- fragment
- assess
- amount
- shortage
- numerous
- minimize
- depth
- meter
- bicentennial
- metric
- percent
- centipede
- geometry
- diameter
- speedometer
- minus
- miniature
- minimum
- incomplete
- multiple
- total
- identical
- medium
- fraction
- decade
- double
- circular
- diagonal

Words Used to Measure Time ③

Words Used to Measure Shapes ④

Words That Tell How Much or What Size ⑭

Words Used to Add and Subtract ⑤

Complete the Groups Write a word from the Word List that completes each group. Some groups are synonyms. Other groups are words that are related to each other.

1 piece, chip, _____

2 single, _____, triple

3 small, _____, large

4 square, rectangular, _____

5 large, huge, _____

Review the Meanings Decide if each sentence is true or false. Write **true** or **false** on the line.

_____ **6** When you draw a triangle, two of your lines are **diagonal**.

_____ **7** A **century** is one hundred years long.

_____ **8** A **speedometer** tells you how long something is.

_____ **9** The **depth** of a lake measures how wide it is from one end to the other.

_____ **10** The **metric** system is a system of colors.

_____ **11** If you make **numerous** mistakes on a test, you will get a perfect score.

_____ **12** The **total** tells how much of something there is.

_____ **13** A **meter** is just over thirty-nine inches long.

_____ **14** A **centipede** has only two legs.

_____ **15** The **amount** tells you what shape something is.

Taking Vocabulary Tests

TEST-TAKING STRATEGY

When taking a test with sentences, read each sentence to yourself. For the first item, look at the answer choices and think of a word that could fill in the blank. Perhaps the word you thought of is one of the answer choices. If it isn't, find the word that best completes the sentence. If you are not sure, take a guess. Don't leave any question blank.

Sample:

Fill in the letter of the answer that best completes the sentence.

A **centipede** is a type of ___.

Ⓐ ruler
Ⓑ coin
Ⓒ bug
Ⓓ measurement

Practice Test   Fill in the letter of the answer that BEST completes each sentence.

1 Something **miniature** is ___.
Ⓐ new
Ⓑ large
Ⓒ small
Ⓓ great

2 A **decade** is ___.
Ⓐ five months
Ⓑ one year
Ⓒ ten years
Ⓓ one hundred years

3 Something **incomplete** is ___.
Ⓐ unfinished
Ⓑ beautiful
Ⓒ long
Ⓓ interesting

4 A **shortage** of something means ___.
Ⓐ too cold
Ⓑ too hot
Ⓒ too much
Ⓓ too little

5 You measure the **diameter** of a ___.
Ⓐ triangle
Ⓑ circle
Ⓒ square
Ⓓ rectangle

6 A **fraction** is a ___.
Ⓐ card
Ⓑ ruler
Ⓒ part
Ⓓ food

7 A **bicentennial** takes place every ___.
Ⓐ two years
Ⓑ ten years
Ⓒ hundred years
Ⓓ two hundred years

8 You **minimize** something that you ___.
Ⓐ want a lot of
Ⓑ make less of
Ⓒ can't hear
Ⓓ measure carefully

9 When you **assess** your work, you ___ it.
Ⓐ judge
Ⓑ write
Ⓒ enjoy
Ⓓ find

10 Things that are **identical** are ___.
Ⓐ colorful
Ⓑ long
Ⓒ full
Ⓓ alike

Play with Language

Find Words Within Words Read each sentence. Look at the underlined word from the Word List. Some of the letters in the word are boldfaced. Rearrange the boldfaced letters to spell a word to complete the sentence. Write the letters of the new word on the lines. The first one is done for you.

1 This isn't a <u>minus</u> sign. It's a plus sign. Add the numbers to get the
<u>s</u> <u>u</u> <u>m</u>.

2 Pay one hundred <u>percent</u> of the ___ ___ ___ ___, or the landlord may tell you to live somewhere else.

3 In <u>geometry</u> class, we studied shapes. Lines, which make up each shape, ___ ___ ___ ___ at certain places.

4 If two people have the same thought, they have an <u>identical</u>
___ ___ ___ ___.

5 With a <u>minimum</u> of four players, we can make two ___ ___ ___ ___ teams.

6 The sun is <u>immense</u>. It just doesn't ___ ___ ___ ___ so big because it is so far away.

7 If you leave ice out for <u>multiple</u> hours, it'll ___ ___ ___ ___.

8 Look at this ___ ___ ___ ___. How many <u>meters</u> tall is it?

9 I found a <u>centipede</u> while I was digging a ___ ___ ___ ___ hole.

10 If you have <u>numerous</u> pens, you have not one, but ___ ___ ___ ___.

Speak It! Try this game. Begin by saying, "If…." The next person ends by saying, "then…." In each part of the sentence, use a word from the Word List in Part 4. For example, "*If* I get one hundred **percent** on my test, *then* I'll get **double** dessert."

PART 1

Context Clues

for Word Wisdom

Standing Up to Unfair Laws:
Rosa Parks

On December 1, 1955, Rosa Parks changed history. African Americans were being treated unfairly on city buses, and in stores, restaurants, and movie theaters. Read this essay to find out what Rosa Parks did.

Rosa Parks worked in a store in Montgomery, Alabama. She was tired from work. She was also tired of the **unjust** laws that treated African American people differently from white people. Rosa Parks decided she would not stand for it any longer.

Rosa Parks was riding home on a bus. The bus had separate sections for white people and African Americans. Rosa Parks was African American. She sat in the white section. A white man got on the bus and demanded that Rosa give her seat to him. Rosa refused.

Rosa had argued with bus drivers before. They had **evicted** her by forcing her to get off the bus. On this day, she didn't want to leave or to give up her seat. The driver acted like an **emperor** by commanding Rosa to get up. Rosa still refused. The driver saw that he couldn't **enforce** the law by himself. He called the police.

The police arrested Rosa. They said she was **violating** the law.

The **regulations** in Alabama said that whites and African Americans should be separate.

News of Parks's arrest spread. People were angry about it. The African American community decided on a **policy** to fight the unfair laws. It would be used throughout the city. African Americans refused to ride city buses. They showed that they weren't going to take unfair treatment any longer.

Rosa Parks was given a **trial** in court. The judge said that she was guilty. Rosa's lawyer believed the decision was wrong. He wanted to take the case to the U.S. Supreme Court. The Supreme Court agreed with Rosa Parks. The Supreme Court said that all **citizens** should be treated equally.

Rosa Parks was a very brave woman. She stood up right at a time when unfair treatment of people **reigned**. Her bravery led to changes that helped all African Americans.

Context Clues Strategy

Look for the Location or Setting

EXAMPLE: The judge used the *gavel* in court to signal that the trial would begin.

CLUE: The words *in court to signal that the trial would begin* tell about the place—the location and setting. This tells where a gavel is used.

Here are steps to figure out the meaning of the word *policy*, which appears in the essay about Rosa Parks.

Read the sentence with the unknown word. Read a sentence or two around it.

The African American community decided on a **policy** *to fight the unfair laws. It would be used throughout the city.*

Look for context clues. What clues can you find about **the Location or Setting?**

The words *throughout the city* tell where the *policy* was used.

Think about the context clues and other helpful information you may already know.

I've never heard the word *policy* before, but it sounds as if the African American community had a plan.

Predict a meaning for the word.

Policy must mean "a plan to get something done."

Check the Word Wisdom Dictionary to be sure of the meaning.

The word *policy* means "a plan of action."

Unlock the Meanings

Practice the Strategy   The word in the box below is from the essay about Rosa Parks on page 182. Use the context clues strategy on page 183 to figure out the meaning of the word.

regulations

Read the sentence that uses the word *regulations*. Read some of the sentences around the word.

Look for context clues. What clues can you find about **the Location or Setting?**

_____

_____

_____

Think about the context clues. What other helpful information do you already know?

_____

_____

_____

Predict a meaning for the word *regulations*.

_____

_____

_____

Check the Word Wisdom Dictionary to be sure of the meaning of the word *regulation*. Write the dictionary definition.

_____

_____

Use Context Clues You have been introduced to two of the boldfaced words from the essay about Rosa Parks. These words have been checked off in the Word List. In the first column, write the other eight words from the Word List. In the second column, use context clues to predict a meaning for each word. Then look up the meaning of the word in the Word Wisdom Dictionary. In the third column, write the dictionary meaning that fits the context.

WORD LIST

unjust	
evict	
emperor	
enforce	
violate	
✔ regulation	
✔ policy	
trial	
citizen	
reign	

	Vocabulary Word	Your Prediction	Dictionary Says
1			
2			
3			
4			
5			
6			
7			
8			

Process the Meanings

WORD LIST

unjust
evict
emperor
enforce
violate
regulation
policy
trial
citizen
reign

Find the Synonyms Match each synonym in the left column with a word from the Word List. Write the vocabulary word in the right column.

Synonym	Vocabulary Word
1 remove	_____
2 law	_____
3 king	_____
4 disobey	_____
5 unfair	_____

Complete the Sentences On the blank line, write the word from the Word List that completes each sentence.

6 Anyone who wants to be president of the United States needs

a good election _____.

7 Someone who was born in Canada is a Canadian

_____.

8 When the war is over, peace will _____

in the land.

9 It is the job of the police to _____

the law.

10 The accused man will have a _____,

and the jury will decide if he is guilty.

Apply What You've Learned

Demonstrate Word Knowledge   Answer the questions.

1 Why might a teacher **evict** a student from the classroom? _____

_____

2 What is a rule that your parents **enforce**? _____

_____

3 What is the role of an **emperor**? _____

_____

4 When is a person given a **trial** in a court? _____

_____

5 What could happen if a person **violates** a traffic law? _____

_____

6 What country are you a **citizen** of? _____

_____

7 How do you feel if you see something **unjust** being done? _____

_____

8 What is your **policy** for getting ready for school every day? _____

_____

9 Why does a society need **regulations**? _____

_____

10 When does peace **reign** among people? _____

_____

 **Write It!**   Write a list of the regulations you would make if you were an emperor. Use several vocabulary words from Part 1.

PART 2 Latin Roots

for Word Wisdom

English Royalty:
Queen Victoria

Victoria was the Queen of England for sixty-four years. No other king or queen ruled longer than she did.

Victoria was only eighteen years old. But she was now the Queen of England. It was 1837. She was not sure how to be a good **ruler**. But she was very smart. And she had a strong spirit. The people in England learned to admire their new queen. They gave her **regal** treatment. This is what a king or queen expected.

Victoria married Prince Albert when she was twenty-one years old. He was from Germany. Albert was very important to the queen. They spent a lot of time at Windsor Castle. The castle is an enormous **fortress**. Strong walls and high towers **fortify** the castle. It has been a home for many kings and queens. In fact, today's **royal** family still uses it. Prince Albert died there. Both he and Victoria are buried there also.

The queen was very upset when her husband died. She did not want to see anyone. She did not want to go outside. In fact, she hid herself for twenty-five years! She talked to her family. She also talked to government people. But she did not want the public to see her. She finally came out in 1887 to celebrate her anniversary. She had been queen for fifty years. The people were happy to see her!

Victoria was a well-liked queen. She was also seen as a successful queen. England won control of many countries during this time. This **imperial** growth was a huge **reinforcement** of England's power. The British **Empire** was the biggest it ever was. India was one country that England ruled. There were many others.

Some experts say that England did not rule India fairly. They say that this **misrule** caused a lot of trouble for India. People in India did not want a distant country to rule them. They fought against it. But England was strong at that time. It kept control of India. People even called Victoria the "**Empress** of India." This meant that she ruled the country. It was a part of her empire. India was not free from England until 1947—forty-six years after Victoria died.

Practice the Context Clues Strategy Here is one of the boldfaced words from the essay on page 188. Use the context clues strategy you learned in Part 1 on page 183 to figure out the meaning of this word.

regal

Read the sentence that uses the word *regal*. Read some of the sentences around the word.

Look for context clues to the word's meaning. What clues showing **the Location or Setting** can you find?

_____

_____

Think about the context clues. What other helpful information do you know?

_____

_____

Predict a meaning for the word *regal*.

_____

_____

Check your Word Wisdom Dictionary to be sure of the meaning of the word *regal*. Which of the meanings for *regal* fits the context?

_____

_____

Many English words come from Latin roots. If you know the meanings of different roots, you can unlock the meanings of new words. Some words you learned in Part 1 have a Latin root. Each root is related to the law.

Latin Root: **fort**
meaning: strong
English word: *enforce*
meaning: to cause to be obeyed

Latin Root: **emp, imp**
meaning: to command
English word: *emperor*
meaning: the male ruler of an empire

Latin Root: **rect**
meaning: to rule; straight
English word: *reign*
meaning: to rule over

WORD LIST

ruler
regal
fortress
fortify
royal
imperial
reinforcement
empire
misrule
empress

Sort by Roots Sort the words in the Word List by their roots. Remember that the spellings of roots can change. The root *rect* can also be spelled *ro*, *rul*, or *reg*. Write each word in the correct column. Think of other words that come from the same Latin roots. Write each word in the correct column.

The Law

Latin Root: fort	Latin Root: emp, imp	Latin Root: rect

Prefix	Meaning	Example
mis-	wrong	**mis-** (wrong) + **rule** (rule) = **misrule**

Use Roots and Prefixes Circle the root and any prefix you find in each boldfaced word below. Remember that spellings of roots can change. Use context clues, roots, and prefixes to write the meaning of the word. Check your definitions in the Word Wisdom Dictionary.

1 I ate a **regal** meal in the fancy restaurant.

_____

2 Guards stand at the entrance of the **imperial** palace.

_____

3 The king **fortified** the palace by building high walls around it.

_____

4 When the hero came to town, he was given a **royal** welcome.

_____

5 This woman, who looks like a queen, is the **empress** of these countries.

_____

6 If troops become tired, **reinforcements** will be sent to help.

_____

7 The ancient **empire** of Rome was very powerful.

_____

8 The judge's decision was wrong; he had **misruled**.

_____

9 Our king is a fair and just **ruler**.

_____

10 The soldiers are safe in the **fortress**.

_____

WORD LIST

- ruler
- regal
- fortress
- fortify
- royal
- imperial
- reinforcement
- empire
- misrule
- empress

Match the Clues Read each clue. On the line, write the word from the Word List that best matches each clue.

1 a female leader _____

2 someone who leads a country _____

3 a protected castle _____

4 a kingdom _____

5 to rule unfairly _____

Use the Words Correctly in Writing Rewrite each sentence in your own words. Include the vocabulary word in parentheses in your sentence.

6 Will the soldiers on the battlefield need help? (reinforcements)

_____

_____

7 We must strengthen the dam before the rain comes. (fortify)

_____

8 We took a tour around the palace that was made for the king and queen. (royal)

_____

9 This red robe and that gold crown are fit for a queen. (regal)

_____

10 The emperor's order arrived this morning. (imperial)

_____

Apply What You've Learned

Demonstrate Word Knowledge Complete the sentences.

1 You would remain in a **fortress** when _____

_____

2 Workers are happy to have **reinforcements** when _____

_____

3 Countries in the same **empire** have the same _____

_____

4 You might get **royal** treatment when _____

_____

5 A person might dress in **regal** clothing when _____

_____

6 A good **ruler** should _____

_____

7 The job of an **empress** is to _____

_____

8 The home of an **imperial** family is probably _____

_____

9 If an umpire **misrules** in a game, fans feel _____

_____

10 Food that is **fortified** with vitamins is _____

_____

Speak It! Imagine that you are a ruler. Make a speech about someone who is a hero in your country. Use several Part 2 vocabulary words.

PART 3 Reference Skills

for Word Wisdom

A Man With His Own Laws:
Napoleon Bonaparte

Some people thought that Napoleon was a great leader. Others thought he was brutal. One thing is for sure. He lived by his own set of rules.

Most people think Napoleon was French. But he wasn't. He was born in Italy. As a young man, he joined the French army. He made his name sound more French. He helped **defend** France many times. Nearby countries often tried to attack France. Napoleon won battle after battle. Then he took over other countries for France.

Egypt was one of these countries. The Egyptian **rebels** put up a good fight. But in the end, Napoleon was **victorious**. He **governed** the part of Egypt that he won. He set up a new government. He brought in new equipment, such as the printing press. He made a health department, and he built hospitals. These things helped the country and its people.

Many of the French people liked Napoleon. Many people admired him because of the battles he won. They even gave him high military **titles**. But Napoleon wanted more.

He took over the French government. He made his own set of laws for the people to follow. He called these laws the Code Napoleon.

Napoleon was soon crowned Emperor of France. He planned a grand **coronation**. He wanted a magnificent ceremony. He asked many people to be there. He had special music, clothes, and jewelry made. He had an artist paint a portrait of the crowning. It was quite a party! The service took place in 1804.

Napoleon often made his own rules. He **dethroned** the King of Spain. Then he had his own brother take the king's place! This is an example of Napoleon's harshness. Eventually, he had control over most of Europe. But soon things changed for Napoleon.

In 1814, Napoleon **surrendered** his throne. A few countries joined together and defeated him. But a year later, Napoleon took his throne back. He became emperor again. But this time he stayed only for a few months. He was taken as a prisoner. He **pleaded** with those who caught him. But no one listened. Napoleon was held **captive** on the island of St. Helena for the rest of his life. He died in 1821.

Practice the Context Clues Strategy Here is one of the boldfaced words from the essay on page 194. Use the context clues strategy you learned in Part 1 on page 183 to figure out the meaning of this word.

coronation

Read the sentence that uses the word *coronation*. Read some of the sentences around the word.

Look for context clues to the word's meaning. What clues showing **the Location or Setting** can you find?

_____

_____

_____

Think about the context clues. What other helpful information do you know?

_____

_____

_____

Predict a meaning for the word *coronation*.

_____

_____

_____

Check your Word Wisdom Dictionary to be sure of the meaning of the word *coronation*. Write the definition here.

_____

_____

_____

🔑 Unlock the Meanings

The Encyclopedia An encyclopedia gives information about many topics. The topics are in ABC order. Once you find your topic, you can read a short article about it. If you are looking for information about a person, look in ABC order by the person's last name.

Encyclopedias often come in sets of books called **volumes.** The volumes are numbered. On every book, you will find which letters of the alphabet that volume covers. For example, if you are looking for information about ants, you would find the information in Volume 1 (abbreviated Vol. 1), if Volume 1 covers the letters A through C.

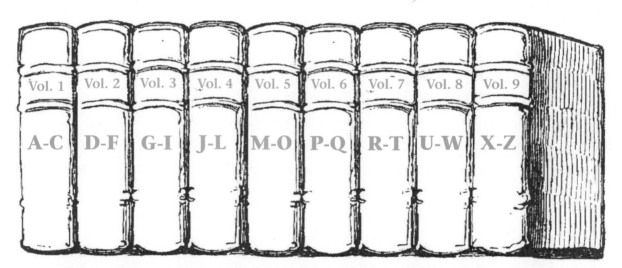

Vol. 1 | Vol. 2 | Vol. 3 | Vol. 4 | Vol. 5 | Vol. 6 | Vol. 7 | Vol. 8 | Vol. 9

A-C D-F G-I J-L M-O P-Q R-T U-W X-Z

Choose the Correct Encyclopedia Volume Use the set of encyclopedia volumes above. Match the topics in the left column with the encyclopedia volume they would be found in. Write your answer on the line in the right column.

1 *The Titanic* _____

2 the Pony Express _____

3 the Venus Flytrap _____

4 Helen Keller _____

5 coronations _____

Find the Meaning
1. Use context clues.
2. Look for a familiar root, prefix, or suffix.
3. If the context or a word part doesn't help, check the dictionary.

Define the Words   Follow the steps above to write the meaning of each boldfaced word. Write 1, 2, or 3 to show which steps you used.

WORD LIST
- defend
- rebel
- victorious
- govern
- title
- coronation
- dethrone
- surrender
- plead
- captive

1 The **rebels** overthrew the evil king.

_____

2 The cat **defended** her kitten from the dog.

_____

3 The troops **surrendered** when they knew they would lose.

_____

4 The **captive** was set free after the war was over.

_____

5 When you speak to the judge, use the **title** "Your Honor."

_____

6 A crown was placed on the new queen's head at the **coronation**.

_____

7 The man who robbed the bank **pleaded** guilty to the crime.

_____

8 The people were unhappy with the king, so they **dethroned** him.

_____

9 The **victorious** army proudly marched home.

_____

10 The mayor **governs** the city.

_____

WORD LIST

defend
rebel
victorious
govern
title
coronation
dethrone
surrender
plead
captive

Choose the Correct Words   Write the word from the Word List that best completes each sentence. You will need to add an ending to one word.

1 "Dr.," "Mrs.," and "Sir" are _____.

2 Don't _____. Keep trying to win.

3 At the king's _____, a jeweled crown was placed on his head.

4 The ruler never expected his servant to turn against him and become a _____.

5 The king is not liked. There's a plan to _____ him.

Replace the Words   Choose the best word from the Word List to take the place of the underlined word. You will have to add an ending to two words.

6 Who will <u>rule</u> the country when the queen dies?

_____

7 The <u>winning</u> team was given a gold medal.

_____

8 The army took five <u>prisoners</u> in the last battle.

_____

9 The navy and the army will do their best to <u>protect</u> the country. _____

10 The man on trial <u>said</u> that he was innocent.

_____

Apply What You've Learned

Demonstrate Word Knowledge Read each sentence. Decide whether it is true or false. Write **true** or **false** on the blank line.

_____ **1** A **rebel** would be a good friend of the king.

_____ **2** A **title** such as "President" or "Mr." is used before a person's name.

_____ **3** When a king is doing a good job, his people will **dethrone** him.

_____ **4** You **surrender** when you are winning.

_____ **5** Someone who did nothing wrong should **plead** guilty in court.

_____ **6** Many people **defend** their right to say what they think.

Complete the Analogies Choose the word that best completes each statement. Write the word on the line.

7 Command is to order as **govern** is to _____.

    a. rule   b. play   c. speak

8 Successful is to unsuccessful as **victorious** is to _____.

    a. happy   b. rich   c. defeated

9 Robber is to thief as **captive** is to _____.

    a. lawyer   b. prisoner   c. jail

10 Ceremony is to award as **coronation** is to _____.

    a. robe   b. crown   c. shoes

Write It! Write a story about a group of rebels who want to dethrone the king of their country. Use as many vocabulary words from Part 3 as you can.

Review

for Word Wisdom

WORD LIST

- unjust
- evict
- emperor
- enforce
- violate
- regulation
- policy
- trial
- citizen
- reign
- ruler
- regal
- fortress
- fortify
- royal
- imperial
- reinforcement
- empire
- misrule
- empress
- defend
- rebel
- victorious
- govern
- title
- coronation
- dethrone
- surrender
- plead
- captive

Sort by Meaning Look at each word in the Word List. Then write the word in the correct column of the chart. Check off each word in the list as you work. The number tells how many words go in that group.

Words That Can Describe Rulers 5	Words That Name Royal Things 9	What a Ruler Can Do 12

Demonstrate Word Knowledge Answer the questions.

1 What are some **regal** things you might find in an **imperial** palace?

_____

2 Why must a king who **misrules** be worried about **rebels**?

_____

3 What might a **ruler** do when people **violate** the rules?

_____

4 What is another word for **regulations** that the police **enforce** and that **citizens** follow?

_____

5 What is the difference between an **emperor** and an **empress**?

_____

6 Why would people want to **dethrone** an **unjust** king?

_____

7 What **title** is given to a woman from a **royal** family at her **coronation**?

_____

8 Why might soldiers in a **fortress** need **reinforcements**?

_____

9 How can a **policy** help a political candidate be **victorious**?

_____

10 Why do people **plead** innocent at a **trial**?

_____

Review

Taking Vocabulary Tests

TEST-TAKING STRATEGY

This test will show how well you know the meaning of the boldfaced words. Read each paragraph carefully. See if you can think of a meaning for the boldfaced word. Then read the answer choices. See if the meaning you thought of is an answer choice. Recheck your answer choice by substituting it for the boldfaced word. Completely fill in the circle of your choice.

Sample:

Our army was caught by surprise when the enemy attacked. During the battle, the enemy army captured five of our soldiers. After the war, our army and their army will trade **captives.**

The word **captives** means ___.
- ○ armies
- ● prisoners
- ○ weapons
- ○ kings

Practice Test   Read each paragraph carefully. Then fill in the circle of the answer choice that BEST completes the sentence.

1   The king is worried about an attack. So he commands his army to **fortify** the castle. The army is working night and day to honor his command.
The word **fortify** means ___.
○ weaken   ○ plan   ○ decorate ○ strengthen

2   The fire department wants to make sure that fires don't start in the school building. It has decided that no candles may be lit in any classroom. This is a new **regulation**.
The word **regulation** means ___.
○ fire   ○ rule   ○ list   ○ problem

3   Our team was losing the game. We knew we had no chance of winning. Still, we refused to **surrender**. We would play until the game was over.
The word **surrender** means ___.
○ give up   ○ complain loudly
○ play more   ○ score goals

4   Charles couldn't find his favorite pen. He accused me of taking it. I had to **defend** myself. I told him that I didn't take it.
The word **defend** means ___.
○ attack   ○ protect ○ hide   ○ pretend

5   This old building is unsafe. People who live in it must find another place to live. The owner of the building will **evict** anyone who doesn't leave.
The word **evict** means ___.
○ pay money to   ○ be angry with
○ force to leave   ○ scream loudly at

Build New Words

Add Suffixes to Change the Words The suffixes *-ion, -ity,* and *-ment* usually have similar meanings. They often mean "the act of" or "the state of." Add the suffixes shown to change each vocabulary word into a new word. You may need to check the spellings in your dictionary. Use the new word in a sentence.

Word	+ Suffix	= New Word	Sentence
evict	-ion		
enforce	-ment		
violate	-ion		
captive	-ity		
rebel	-ion		

Speak It! Imagine that you are a rebel in an empire ruled by a bad emperor. Give a speech that will persuade others to join you in your plan to dethrone the bad emperor. Use as many words from this unit as you can.

W!Rd Wisdom Dictionary

PRONUNCIATION KEY

/ă/	pat
/ā/	pay
/â/	care
/ä/	father
/är/	far
/ĕ/	pet
/ē/	be
/ĭ/	pit
/ī/	pie
/îr/	pier
/ŏ/	mop
/ō/	toe
/ô/	paw, for
/oi/	noise
/ou/	out
/o͝o/	look
/o͞o/	boot
/ŭ/	cut
/ûr/	urge
/th/	thin
/th/	this
/hw/	what
/zh/	vision
/ə/	about
	item
	pencil
	gallop
	circus
/ər/	butter

A

a•cross /ə krôs′ *or* ə krŏs′/ *prep.* from one side to another. *I walked across the street.*

ad•mit[1] /ăd mĭt′/ *v.* **ad•mit•ted, ad•mit•ting, ad•mits.** to agree that something is true. *I admit that Tom's answer is better than mine.*

ad•mit[2] /ăd mĭt′/ *v.* **ad•mit•ted, ad•mit•ting, ad•mits.** to let enter. *These tickets will admit two to the basketball game.*

ad•vice /ăd vīs′/ *n.* an opinion or suggestion about what someone should do. *The babysitter asked for advice about feeding the children.*

af•ford /ə fôrd′/ *v.* **af•ford•ed, af•ford•ing, af•fords.** to be able to pay for something. *My parents said that we can afford a new car.* —**af•ford•a•ble** *adj.*

af•ford•a•ble /ə fôr′ də bəl/ *adj.* reasonably priced. *This shirt is nice, and it's affordable.*

ag•ri•cul•ture /ăg′ rĭ kŭl′ chər/ *n.* the science of farming. *The states of Illinois and Iowa are known for agriculture.*
  —**ag•ri•cul•tur•al** *adj.*
  —**ag•ri•cul•tur•al•ly** *adv.*
  —**ag•ri•cul•tur•ist** *n.*

al•bum[1] /ăl′ bəm/ *n.* a book in which photographs are placed. *My mother made a photograph album for each child in the family.*

al•bum[2] /ăl′ bəm/ *n.* a turntable record. *My mom has an album collection from the 1970s and 1980s.*

a•lert[1] /ə lûrt′/ *adj.* watchful. *An alert police officer can sometimes stop a crime before it begins.*

a•lert[2] /ə lûrt′/ *v.* **a•lert•ed, a•lert•ing, a•lerts.** to warn. *The firefighter will alert the neighbors about the fire on the corner.*

a•mount[1] /ə mount′/ *n.* a quantity or measure. *A small amount of snow fell during the night.*

a•mount[2] /ə mount′/ *v.* **a•mount•ed, a•mount•ing, a•mounts.** to add up in number or quantity. *The cost of the pens and paper will amount to ten dollars.*

an•i•ma•tion /ăn′ ə mā′ shən/ *n.* liveliness. *The little girl's animation showed how much she enjoyed the game.*

an•nounce[1] /ə nouns′/ *v.* **an•nounced, an•nounc•ing, an•nounc•es.** to say something loudly or publicly; to make known. *The judges will announce the winners.*

an•nounce² /ə nouns′/ *v.* **an•nounced, an•nounc•ing, an•nounc•es.** to introduce the arrival of. *Our teacher will announce the guest speaker.*

an•nounce•ment /ə nouns′ mənt/ *n.* a statement that is made aloud in front of people. *The announcement about the first day of school was in the paper.*

an•nounc•er /ə noun′ sər/ *n.* a person who brings something to public attention. *The radio announcer will read the news.*

ap•pli•ca•tion /ăp′ lĭ kā′ shən/ *n.* a written request. *My brother filled out an application for a job.*

ap•proach¹ /ə prōch′/ *v.* **ap•proached, ap•proach•ing, ap•proach•es.** to come near. *The ambulance approached the scene of the accident.*

ap•proach² /ə prōch′/ *n., pl.* **ap•proach•es.** the act of moving closer. *The airplane made a smooth approach to the landing field.*

ar•rest /ə rĕst′/ *v.* **ar•rest•ed, ar•rest•ing, ar•rests.** to take as a prisoner. *The police arrested the jewelry thief.*

ar•ti•cle¹ /är′ tĭ kəl/ *n.* an individual thing. *We bought three new articles of clothing.*

ar•ti•cle² /är′ tĭ kəl/ *n.* a report; a piece of writing. *There was an article about our school in the newspaper.*

as•cend /ə sĕnd′/ *v.* **as•cend•ed, as•cend•ing, as•cends.** to go up. *The airplane ascended above the clouds.* —**as•cen•sion** *n.*

as•sem•ble /ə sĕm′ bəl/ *v.* **as•sem•bled, as•sem•bling, as•sem•bles.** to put the parts together. *Jeremy likes to assemble model planes.*

as•sem•bly¹ /ə sĕm′ blē/ *n., pl.* **as•sem•blies.** a group gathered for a common reason. *Our school assembly will be in the gymnasium.*

as•sem•bly² /ə sĕm′ blē/ *n., pl.* **as•sem•blies.** the process of putting parts together. *Directions were included for the bike's assembly.*

as•sess¹ /ə sĕs′/ *v.* **as•sessed, as•sess•ing, as•sess•es.** to charge a fine or special payment. *The police officer assessed the driver fifty dollars for speeding.* —**as•sess•a•ble** *adj.*

as•sess² /ə sĕs′/ *v.* **as•sessed, as•sess•ing, as•sess•es.** to evaluate or judge. *The coach uses practice to assess the players' strengths.* —**as•sess•a•ble** *adj.*

as•sis•tance /ə sĭs′ təns/ *n.* help. *I needed assistance hanging the poster.*

as•sis•tant /ə sĭs′ tənt/ *n.* a helper. *The teacher needed an assistant to help during math.*

at•ten•tion /ə tĕn′ shən/ *n.* concentration; notice. *The loud fire alarm got my attention.* —**at•ten•tive** *adj.*

au•thor /ô′ thər/ *n.* the writer of a book, story, or play. *Dr. Seuss is a famous author of children's books.*

au•to•graph¹ /ô′ tə grăf′/ *n.* a signature of a famous person. *I have the autograph of a famous baseball player.* —**au•to•graph•ic** *adj.* —**au•to•graph•i•cal** *adj.* —**au•to•graph•i•cal•ly** *adv.*

au•to•graph² /ô′ tə grăf′/ *v.* **au•to•graphed, au•to•graph•ing, au•to•graphs.** to write one's name on. *The songwriter always autographs his albums.* —**au•to•graph•ic** *adj.* —**au•to•graph•i•cal** *adj.* —**au•to•graph•i•cal•ly** *adv*

B

bi•cen•ten•ni•al /bī′ sĕn tĕn′ ē əl/ *n.* a 200th anniversary. *Our town will celebrate its bicentennial this year.*

bi•ol•o•gy /bī ŏl′ ə jē/ *n., pl.* **bi•ol•o•gies.** the study of living things. *We studied frogs in biology class.* —**bi•ol•o•gist** *n.*

brain•storm¹ /brān′ stôrm′/ *n.* a sudden idea. *The girl had a brainstorm about how to solve the problem.*

brain•storm² /brān′ stôrm′/ *v.* **brain•stormed, brain•storm•ing, brain•storms.** to bring up ideas together. *Let's brainstorm about where to go on a class trip.* —**brain•storm•er** *n.*

budge /bŭj/ *v.* **budged, budg•ing, budg•es.** to move a little bit. *We could not budge the heavy box.*

C

cap•tion¹ /kăp′ shən/ *n.* the words telling about a picture. *Read the caption under the photograph to find out who is in it.*

cap•tion² /kăp′ shən/ *v.* **cap•tioned, cap•tion•ing, cap•tions.** to furnish a caption or an explanation for. *Be sure to caption your drawings.*

cap•tive /kăp′ tĭv/ *n.* a person held as a prisoner. *The captive was in handcuffs.*

cap•tiv•i•ty /kăp tĭv′ ĭ tē/ *n., pl.* **cap•tiv•i•ties.** the state of being held as a prisoner. *The prisoner was in captivity for most of his life.*

cap•ture¹ /kăp′ chər/ *v.* **cap•tured, cap•tur•ing, cap•tures.** to get hold of someone or something. *The zookeeper captured the animal after it escaped.*

cap•ture² /kăp′ chər/ *n.* the act of capturing. *The capture of the thief brought peace to the community.*

cen•ti•pede /sĕn′ tə pēd′/ *n.* a small, worm-like creature with many body segments, each with a pair of legs. *A centipede crept down the wall.*

cen•tu•ry /sĕn′ chə rē/ *n., pl.* **cen•tu•ries.** a period of one hundred years. *Each century brings many new discoveries.*

chap•ter /chăp′ tər/ *n.* a section of a book. *I've reached the tenth chapter of my book.*

chase¹ /chās/ *v.* **chased, chas•ing, chas•es.** to follow quickly. *The girl chased her dog down the hill.*

chase² /chās/ *n.* the act of following quickly. *We joined the chase to catch the puppy.*

cir•cu•lar /sûr′ kyə lər/ *adj.* shaped like a circle. *There was a circular pool in the backyard.* —**cir•cu•lar•ly** *adv.* —**cir•cu•lar•i•ty** *n.*

cit•i•zen /sĭt′ ĭ zən/ *n.* a loyal resident of a country. *My friend is a citizen of Australia.*

clus•ter¹ /klŭs′ tər/ *v.* **clus•tered, clus•ter•ing, clus•ters.** to gather. *The children clustered around the clown.*

clus•ter² /klŭs′ tər/ *n.* similar things grouped together. *The cluster of grapes looked lovely.*

com•merce /kŏm′ ərs/ *n.* business. *Most commerce stops on important holidays.*

com•mer•cial¹ /kə mûr′ shəl/ *adj.* having to do with business. *The commercial area of our town is near a large park.* —**com•mer•cial•ly** *adv.*

com•mer•cial² /kə mûr′ shəl/ *n.* an advertisement on radio or television. *We watched a commercial for the new store.*

com•mu•ni•cate /kə myo͞o′ nĭ kāt′/ *v.* **com•mu•ni•cat•ed, com•mu•ni•cat•ing, com•mu•ni•cates.** to speak or share ideas with someone. *I communicate with my friends by e-mail.*

com•pass /kŭm′ pəs or kŏm′ pəs/ *n., pl.* **com•pass•es.** a tool that shows direction. *The campers used a compass to find the trail.*

com•plain /kəm plān′/ *v.* **com•plained, com•plain•ing, com•plains.** to express negative feelings. *The students never complain about pizza for lunch.*

com•plain•er /kəm plān′ ər/ *n.* a person who expresses negative feelings. *The complainer had nothing positive to say.*

com•ple•tion /kəm plē′ shən/ *n.* the end or finish. *At the completion of the lesson there is a test.*

con•tem•po•rar•y¹ /kən tĕm′ pə rĕr′ ē/ *adj.* modern or current. *Our orchestra plays some contemporary music.* —**con•tem•po•rar•i•ly** *adv.*

con•tem•po•rar•y² /kən tĕm′ pə rĕr′ ē/ *n., pl.* **con•tem•po•rar•ies.** of the same period of time. *Thomas Edison and Henry Ford were contemporaries.*

cor•o•na•tion /kôr′ ə nā′ shən or kŏr ə nā′ shən/ *n.* a ceremony for crowning a king or a queen. *People from around the world attended the queen's coronation.*

cre•ate /krē āt′/ *v.* **cre•at•ed, cre•at•ing, cre•ates.** to construct; to make. *Our neighbor created a garden to attract butterflies.*

PRONUNCIATION KEY	
/ă/	pat
/ā/	pay
/â/	care
/ä/	father
/är/	far
/ĕ/	pet
/ē/	be
/ĭ/	pit
/ī/	pie
/îr/	pier
/ŏ/	mop
/ō/	toe
/ô/	paw, for
/oi/	noise
/ou/	out
/o͝o/	look
/o͞o/	boot
/ŭ/	cut
/ûr/	urge
/th/	thin
/th/	this
/hw/	what
/zh/	vision
/ə/	about
	item
	pencil
	gallop
	circus
/ər/	butter

cre•a•tion /krē ā′ shən/ *n.* something constructed or made. *The student displayed his creation at the science fair.*

crea•ture /krē′ chər/ *n.* a living being, especially an animal. *The rabbit living in our backyard is an adorable creature.*

cross•road /krôs′ rōd′ *or* krŏs′ rōd′/ *n.* a road crossing another road. *The farmers met at the crossroad with their equipment.*

cross•walk /krôs′ wôk′ *or* krŏs′ wôk′/ *n.* a place marked on the street where people can cross. *Look both ways before you enter the crosswalk.*

cruise[1] /krōōz/ *v.* **cruised, cruis•ing, cruis•es.** to travel in an unhurried way. *We cruised along the coast of Maine.*

cruise[2] /krōōz/ *n.* a voyage for pleasure. *My aunt is going on a cruise around the world.*

cur•ren•cy /kûr′ ən sē *or* kŭr′ ən sē/ *n., pl.* **cur•ren•cies.** money used in a particular country. *The United States currency is the dollar.*

D

da•ta /dā′ tə *or* dăt′ ə/ *n., pl. of* **da•tum.** information; facts. *I need some data for my report.*

de•bate[1] /dĭ bāt′/ *v.* **de•bat•ed, de•bat•ing, de•bates.** to think about. *I will debate which street to take to the mall.* —**de•bat•er** *n.*

de•bate[2] /dĭ bāt′/ *v.* **de•bat•ed, de•bat•ing, de•bates.** to present arguments back and forth. *Our parents will debate the issue of school uniforms with the school board.* —**de•bat•er** *n.*

de•bate[3] /dĭ bāt′/ *n.* a contest in which teams argue for or against something. *The judges decided that our team won the debate.*

dec•ade /dĕk′ ād′/ *n.* a period of ten years. *Our house was built a decade ago.*

de•com•pose /dē′ kəm pōz′/ *v.* **de•com•posed, de•com•pos•ing, de•com•pos•es.** to break down; to decay. *The leaves on the ground decompose during the winter.* —**de•com•pos•a•ble** *adj.*

ded•i•ca•tion[1] /dĕd′ ĭ kā′ shən/ *n.* service and time given to something important. *She shows a lot of dedication to her studies.*

ded•i•ca•tion[2] /dĕd′ ĭ kā′ shən/ *n.* a ceremony to honor something. *The dedication of the new library is next week.*

de•fend /dĭ fĕnd′/ *v.* **de•fend•ed, de•fend•ing, de•fends.** to guard or protect. *Our dog defends us with loud barking.* —**de•fend•a•ble** *adj.* —**de•fend•er** *n.*

de•fine /dĭ fīn′/ *v.* **de•fined, de•fin•ing, de•fines.** to give the exact meaning. *The assignment was to define ten vocabulary words.* —**de•fin•a•ble** *adj.* —**de•fin•a•bly** *adv.* —**de•fine•ment** *n.*

def•i•nite /dĕf′ ə nĭt/ *adj.* certain. *It is definite that we will visit my grandparents next week.* —**def•i•nite•ly** *adv.* —**def•i•nite•ness** *n.*

de•liv•er /dĭ lĭv′ ər/ *v.* **de•liv•ered, de•liv•er•ing, de•liv•ers.** to take to a place or person. *The mail carrier will deliver the package today.*

de•liv•er•y /dĭ lĭv′ ə rē/ *n., pl.* **de•liv•er•ies.** something brought or transported to a place. *The postman left his delivery at the front door.*

de•mand[1] /dĭ mănd′/ *v.* **de•mand•ed, de•mand•ing, de•mands.** to ask for; to claim. *Tom will demand payment for the work that he did.* —**de•mand•a•ble** *adj.* —**de•mand•er** *n.*

de•mand[2] /dĭ mănd′/ *n.* something asked for. *The workers' demand for better pay was accepted.*

de•part /dĭ pärt′/ *v.* **de•part•ed, de•part•ing, de•parts.** to leave. *The train will depart from the downtown station.*

de•par•ture /dĭ pär′ chər/ *n.* the act of leaving. *Our flight's time of departure was ten o'clock.*

depth /dĕpth/ *n.* deepness. *We don't know the depth of the water in the lake.*

de•scribe /dĭ skrīb′/ *v.* **de•scribed, de•scrib•ing, de•scribes.** to tell about; to explain. *The motorist described the accident to the police officer.* —**de•scrib•a•ble** *adj.* —**de•scrib•er** *n.*

de•throne /dē thrōn′/ *v.* **de•throned, de•thron•ing, de•thrones.** to remove from a position of power. *The people dethroned their cruel king.* —**de•throne•ment** *n.*

di•ag•o•nal¹ /dī ăg′ ə nəl/ *adj.* slanting. *He drew diagonal lines across his paper.* —**di•ag•o•nal•ly** *adv.*

di•ag•o•nal² /dī ăg′ ə nəl/ *n.* a segment of a slanted line. *Start your diagonal at the top right corner of your paper.*

di•a•gram¹ /dī′ ə grăm′/ *n.* a drawing that explains something. *The diagram showed where the treasure was buried.*

di•a•gram² /dī′ ə grăm′/ *v.* **di•a•grammed, di•a•gram•ming, di•a•grams** *or* **di•a•gramed, di•a•gram•ing, di•a•grams.** to show by drawing. *The teacher diagrammed the class seating plan.* —**di•a•gram•ma•ble** *adj.* —**di•a•gram•mat•ic** *adj.* —**di•a•gram•mat•ic•al•ly** *adv.*

di•am•e•ter /dī ăm′ ĭ tər/ *n.* the distance across a circle measured through its center point. *Measure the diameter of that large round table.*

dic•ta•tion¹ /dĭk tā′ shən/ *n.* the act of saying something to another person who will write it. *The teacher gave dictation of the spelling words for the class to write on paper.*

dic•ta•tion² /dĭk tā′ shən/ *n.* material written down after another person said it. *The judge read the dictation of the witness's statement.*

dic•tion /dĭk′ shən/ *n.* how a person speaks or writes; word choice. *The speaker's diction was clear and easy to understand.*

di•gest¹ /dī jĕst′ or dĭ jĕst′/ *v.* **di•gest•ed, di•gest•ing, di•gests.** to break down food so it can be used. *We can digest some foods more easily than others.*

di•gest² /dī′ jĕst′/ *n.* previously published material produced in condensed form. *A digest of the author's works was published recently.*

dis•cuss /dĭ skŭs′/ *v.* **dis•cussed, dis•cuss•ing, dis•cuss•es.** to talk about. *I discuss my homework with my father every night.*

dis•play¹ /dĭ splā′/ *v.* **dis•played, dis•play•ing, dis•plays.** to show. *The boy will display his paintings at the art show.*

dis•play² /dĭ splā′/ *n.* a showing to the public. *We saw a beautiful display of jewelry at the store.*

dis•sect /dĭ sĕkt′ or dī sĕkt′ or dī′ sĕkt′/ *v.* **dis•sect•ed, dis•sect•ing, dis•sects.** to cut apart and study. *The students dissected different kinds of leaves to compare them.*

dis•tract /dĭ străkt′/ *v.* **dis•tract•ed, dis•tract•ing, dis•tracts.** to take someone's attention away. *Please do not distract me when I am driving.* —**dis•trac•tive** *adj.* —**dis•tract•ing•ly** *adv.*

dou•ble¹ /dŭb′ əl/ *adj.* twice as much. *She had a double helping of vegetables.*

dou•ble² /dŭb′ əl/ *n.* a person or thing that looks like another. *He is a double of his dad in both looks and actions.*

dou•ble³ /dŭb′ əl/ *v.* **dou•bled, dou•bling, dou•bles.** to make twice as much. *He wants to double his score in the next game.*

ed•it /ĕd′ ĭt/ *v.* **ed•it•ed, ed•it•ing, ed•its.** to correct written material. *My friend will edit my paper before I turn it in.*

e•di•tion /ĭ dĭsh′ ən/ *n.* the form or version of a published work. *Did you get the hard-cover edition of the book?*

ed•i•to•ri•al /ĕd′ ĭ tôr′ ē əl or ĕd′ ĭ tōr′ ē əl/ *n.* an article giving someone's opinion. *I wrote an editorial for the newspaper.*

em•per•or /ĕm′ pər ər/ *n.* the male ruler of an empire. *The emperor ruled during a time of peace.* —**em•per•or•ship** *n.*

em•pire /ĕm′ pīr′/ *n.* a group of territories with one ruler. *It took large armies to build an empire.*

em•ploy•er /ĕm ploi′ ər/ *n.* one that pays others to work. *The employer is kind to his workers.*

em•ploy•ment /ĕm ploi′ mənt/ *n.* paid work. *My father found employment as a plumber.*

em•press /ĕm′ prĭs/ *n., pl.* **em•press•es.** the female ruler of an empire; wife of the emperor. *The empress had many people to wait on her.*

/ă/	pat
/ā/	pay
/â/	care
/ä/	father
/är/	far
/ĕ/	pet
/ē/	be
/ĭ/	pit
/ī/	pie
/îr/	pier
/ŏ/	mop
/ō/	toe
/ô/	paw, for
/oi/	noise
/ou/	out
/ŏŏ/	look
/ōō/	boot
/ŭ/	cut
/ûr/	urge
/th/	thin
/*th*/	this
/hw/	what
/zh/	vision
/ə/	about
	item
	pencil
	gallop
	circus
/ər/	butter

en•force /ĕn fôrs′ *or* ĕn fōrs′/ *v.* **en•forced, en•forc•ing, en•forc•es.** to make sure a rule or law is obeyed. *Police officers enforce traffic regulations.* —**en•force•a•ble** *adj.* —**en•force•ment** *n.* —**en•forc•er** *n.*

en•vi•ron•ment /ĕn vī′ rən mənt/ *n.* the conditions that affect the growth of living things. *Living things grow better in an unpolluted environment.* —**en•vi•ron•men•tal** *adj.* —**en•vi•ron•men•tal•ly** *adv.*

ep•i•sode /ep′ ĭ sōd′/ *n.* an event that is part of a series; an incident. *We watched the last episode of the series on television.*

es•cape[1] /ĭ skāp′/ *v.* **es•caped, es•cap•ing, es•capes.** to get free. *My gerbil escaped from its cage.* —**es•ca•pa•ble** *adj.* —**es•ca•per** *n.*

es•cape[2] /ĭ skāp′/ *n.* the act of getting free. *The prisoner's escape was front-page news.*

es•pe•cial•ly /ĕ spĕsh′ ə lē/ *adv.* particularly; exceptionally. *The neighbors were especially kind when my brother was in the hospital.*

es•tab•lish /ĭ stăb′ lĭsh/ *v.* **es•tab•lished, es•tab•lish•ing, es•tab•lish•es.** to set up. *Our school will establish a fund to help the poor in our area.*

es•tab•lish•ment /ĭ stăb′ lĭsh mənt/ *n.* something set up; an organized group. *That business establishment has been around for decades.*

e•ven•tu•al[1] /ĭ vĕn′ chōō əl/ *adj.* occurring in the unknown future. *The eventual collapse of the shaky structure will not surprise anyone.*

e•ven•tu•al[2] /ĭ vĕn′ chōō əl/ *adj.* final. *The eventual success of the movie was a surprise.*

e•ven•tu•al•ly /ĭ vĕn′ chōō ə lē/ *adv.* finally. *The train will eventually get to another station.*

e•vict /ĭ vĭkt′/ *v.* **e•vict•ed, e•vict•ing, e•victs.** to force someone to leave. *The landlord evicted the family from the apartment.*

e•vic•tion /ĭ vĭk′ shən/ *n.* the act of being forced to leave. *The company's eviction forced them to find a new office.*

ev•i•dent /ĕv′ ĭ dənt/ *adj.* clear; apparent. *It was evident to us that snow was coming.* —**ev•i•dent•ly** *adv.*

ex•am•ple /ĭg zăm′ pəl/ *n.* a sample; an illustration. *The class was given an example of handwriting to copy.*

ex•ist /ĭg zĭst′/ *v.* **ex•ist•ed, ex•ist•ing, ex•ists.** to be alive. *Some plants cannot exist in a cold climate.*

ex•pe•ri•ence[1] /ĭk spîr′ ē əns/ *n.* something a person does or goes through. *Our new student told of her experience of moving across the country.*

ex•pe•ri•ence[2] /ĭk spîr′ ē əns/ *n.* knowledge or skill gained from doing something. *We hired a painter with experience to paint our house.*

ex•pe•ri•ence[3] /ĭk spîr′ ē əns/ *v.* **ex•per•i•enced, ex•per•i•enc•ing, ex•per•i•enc•es.** to go through something; to live through. *The boy experienced the excitement of winning the prize.*

ex•per•i•ment[1] /ĭk spĕr′ ə mənt/ *n.* a scientific test. *We performed an experiment in our science class.* —**ex•per•i•ment•er** *n.*

ex•per•i•ment[2] /ĭk spĕr′ ə mənt/ *v.* **ex•per•i•ment•ed, ex•per•i•ment•ing, ex•per•i•ments.** to conduct a test. *We experimented with different kinds of grass before planting a new lawn.* —**ex•per•i•ment•er** *n.*

ex•pert[1] /ĕk′ spûrt′/ *n.* a person with great knowledge or skill in a particular field. *Lawyers are experts in law.*

ex•pert[2] /ĕk′ spûrt *or* ĭk spûrt′/ *adj.* having great knowledge after being trained. *An expert chef worked at the restaurant.* —**ex•pert•ly** *adv.* —**ex•pert•ness** *n.*

ex•per•tise /ĕk′ spûr tēz′/ *n.* specialized skill or knowledge. *We needed the expertise of a bricklayer to build our house.*

ex•press /ĭk sprĕs′/ *v.* **ex•pressed, ex•press•ing, ex•press•es.** to show what you feel or think. *The flute player expressed her feelings with her music.* —**ex•press•i•ble** *adj.* —**ex•press•er** *n.*

ex•tinct /ĭk stĭngkt′/ *adj.* no longer living. *We saw an exhibit about extinct animals at the zoo.*

ex•tin•guish /ĭk stĭng′ gwĭsh/ v.
**ex•tin•guished, ex•tin•guish•ing,
ex•tin•guish•es.** to put out or to get rid of.
*You must extinguish the candle flame
before you go to bed.*

fad /făd/ n. a fashion, interest, or practice that
lasts for a short period of time. *Bell-bottom
jeans were a fad in the seventies.*

fas•ci•nate /făs′ ə nāt′/ v. **fas•ci•nat•ed,
fas•ci•nat•ing, fas•ci•nates.** to attract and
hold the attention of. *Baseball games
always fascinate me.*

fi•nal[1] /fī′ nəl/ adj. last. *She made a basket
in the final moments of the game.*
—fin•al•ly adv.

fi•nal[2] /fī′ nəl/ n. the last in a series. *Our team
was in the final game of the playoffs.*

fi•nal•ist /fī′ nə lĭst/ n. a person who
competes in the last session of a contest.
*My friend was a finalist in the piano
competition.*

flo•ral /flôr′ əl or flōr′ əl/ adj. having to do
with flowers. *The bride had a beautiful
floral bouquet.*

flo•rist /flôr′ ĭst or flōr′ ĭst/ n. a person who
sells plants and flowers. *I ordered some
red and white carnations from the florist.*

flour•ish /flûr′ ĭsh or flŭr′ ĭsh/ v. **flour•ished,
flour•ish•ing, flour•ish•es.** to grow and do
well. *A plant will flourish if it is cared for
properly.*

flow•er•ing /flou′ ər ĭng/ adj. producing
flowers. *We have a spectacular flowering
tree in our backyard.*

for•ti•fy[1] /fôr′ tə fī′/ v. **for•ti•fied,
for•ti•fy•ing, for•ti•fies.** to make stronger
or more secure. *The people can fortify
their village by building walls around it.*
—for•ti•fi•a•ble adj. **—for•ti•fi•er** n.

for•ti•fy[2] /fôr′ tə fī′/ v. **for•ti•fied,
for•ti•fy•ing, for•ti•fies.** to strengthen. *The
healthy meal will fortify you for the race.*
—for•ti•fi•a•ble adj. **—for•ti•fi•er** n.

for•tress /fôr′ trĭs/ n., pl. **for•tress•es.** a large
fort or place that is a stronghold against
attack. *A castle was built to serve as a
fortress.*

frac•tion /frăk′ shən/ n. a small part. *The
students who attended the picnic were just
a fraction of the class.*

frag•ment[1] /frăg′ mənt/ n. a piece broken off.
We dug up a fragment of old pottery.

frag•ment[2] /frăg′ mənt/ v. **frag•ment,
frag•ment•ing, frag•ments.** to break into
pieces. *The glass will fragment if you
drop it.*

fre•quent[1] /frē′ kwənt/ adj. occurring often.
My aunt is a frequent visitor to our house.
—fre•quent•ly adv.

fre•quent[2] /frē kwĕnt′ or frē′ kwənt/ v.
fre•quent•ed, fre•quent•ing, fre•quents.
to visit often. *I frequent the neighborhood
ballpark.* **—fre•quent•ness** n.

ge•om•e•try /jē ŏm′ ĭ trē/ n., pl.
ge•om•e•tries. the mathematical study of
lines, shapes, surfaces, angles, and solids.
Geometry was her favorite kind of math.

glance /glăns/ v. **glanced, glanc•ing,
glanc•es.** to look at quickly. *I glanced out
the window as the school bus drove by.*

glide /glīd/ v. **glid•ed, glid•ing, glides.**
to move smoothly. *The skiers glide down
the mountain slope.*

goal /gōl/ n. the aim or purpose. *My goal is
to get good grades.*

gov•ern /gŭv′ ərn/ v. **gov•erned, gov•ern•ing,
gov•erns.** to make and enforce laws; to
rule or control. *It is a big responsibility to
govern a state.* **—gov•ern•a•ble** adj.

gram•mar /grăm′ ər/ n. the rules a language
has for making sentences. *Our teacher
gives a lesson in grammar every day.*

H

hu•mor•ous /hyōō′ mər əs/ *adj.* funny. *The joke was not very humorous.* —**hu•mor•ous•ly** *adv.* —**hu•mor•ous•ness** *n.*

I

i•den•ti•cal /ī dĕn′ tĭ kəl/ *adj.* exactly the same. *The girls wore identical dresses.* —**i•den•ti•cal•ly** *adv.* —**i•den•ti•cal•ness** *n.*

im•me•di•ate /ĭ mē′ dē ĭt/ *adj.* happening or occurring at once. *I asked for the immediate delivery of the package.* —**im•med•i•ate•ness** *n.*

im•me•di•ate•ly /ĭ mē′ dē ĭt lē/ *adv.* instantly; without delay; promptly. *The ambulance arrived immediately.*

im•mense /ĭ mĕns′/ *adj.* huge. *The new shopping mall is immense.* —**im•mense•ly** *adv.* —**im•mense•ness** *n.*

im•pe•ri•al /ĭm pîr′ ē əl/ *adj.* relating to an empire or its ruler. *The region's imperial gardens were open to the public.* —**im•pe•ri•al•ly** *adv.*

in•an•i•mate /ĭn ăn′ ə mĭt/ *adj.* not living. *Toys are inanimate objects.* —**in•an•i•mate•ly** *adv.* —**in•an•i•mate•ness** *n.*

in•com•plete /ĭn′ kəm plēt′/ *adj.* not finished. *His homework was incomplete when he took it to class.* —**in•com•plete•ly** *adv.* —**in•com•plete•ness** *n.*

in•def•i•nite /ĭn dĕf′ ə nĭt/ *adj.* not clear or certain. *She was indefinite about going to the party.* —**in•def•i•nite•ly** *adv.* —**in•def•i•nite•ness** *n.*

in•fest /ĭn fĕst′/ *v.* **in•fest•ed, in•fest•ing, in•fests.** to appear in large numbers and harm something. *Weeds infested our garden while we were away.* —**in•fes•ta•tion** *n.*

in•fi•nite /ĭn′ fə nĭt/ *adj.* without an end. *Outer space is infinite.* —**in•fi•nite•ly** *adv.* —**in•fi•nite•ness** *n.*

in•scribe /ĭn skrīb′/ *v.* **in•scribed, in•scrib•ing, in•scribes.** to write, print, or engrave on an object. *I asked the jeweler to inscribe my name on the bracelet.* —**in•scrib•er** *n.*

in•ter•cept /ĭn′ tər sĕpt′/ *v.* **in•ter•cept•ed, in•ter•cept•ing, in•ter•cepts.** to stop or interrupt the progress of. *The teacher intercepted the note before it got to me.* —**in•ter•cep•tion** *n.*

in•ter•cep•tor /ĭn′ tər sĕp′ tər/ *n.* one who stops or interrupts the progress of something. *An interceptor kept the message from reaching me.*

in•ven•tive /ĭn vĕn′ tĭv/ *adj.* skillful at creating new things; creative. *We saw many inventive ideas at the science fair.*

in•ven•tor /ĭn vĕn′ tər/ *n.* a person who creates a new thing from an idea. *Alexander Graham Bell is the inventor of the telephone.*

is•sue[1] /ĭsh′ ōō/ *n.* an item or set of printed materials. *Have you seen the latest issue of this magazine?*

is•sue[2] /ĭsh′ ōō/ *n.* a topic that is discussed. *The principal talked about the issue of safety on the playground.*

is•sue[3] /ĭsh′ ōō/ *v.* **is•sued, is•su•ing, is•sues.** to go or come out. *Smoke issued from the burning house.*

J

job•less /jŏb′ lĭs/ *adj.* not having a job. *My uncle was jobless for three months.*

L

la•bor[1] /lā′ bər/ *n.* hard work. *Seeing the new fence made all their labor worthwhile.*

la•bor[2] /lā′ bər/ *v.* **la•bored, la•bor•ing, la•bors.** to work. *The workers labor in the orchard picking peaches.* —**la•bor•er** *n.*

loan[1] /lōn/ *n.* money borrowed that has to be paid back. *Will you need a loan for new skates?*

loan[2] /lōn/ *v.* **loaned, loan•ing, loans.** to lend something that has to be returned. *My friend loaned a book to me.*

lurch /lûrch/ *v.* **lurched, lurch•ing, lurch•es.** to move suddenly. *We watched the hawk lurch toward the mouse.*

M

mar•ket¹ /mär′ kĭt/ *v.* **mar•ket•ed, mar•ket•ing, mar•kets.** to make available for sale. *The store owner markets new shoes.* —**mar•ket•er** *n.*

mar•ket² /mär′ kĭt/ *n.* a place where items are offered for sale. *My grandmother walks to the market every day.*

me•chan•i•cal /mĭ kăn′ ĭ kəl/ *adj.* involving machines or tools. *Repairing bicycles takes mechanical skills.* —**me•chan•i•cal•ly** *adv.*

mech•a•nize /měk′ ə nīz′/ *v.* **mech•a•nized, mech•a•niz•ing, mech•a•niz•es.** to provide machinery. *The Industrial Revolution mechanized factories.*

me•di•um¹ /mē′ dē əm/ *adj.* of middle size or amount. *She needed a sweater of medium size.*

me•di•um² /mē′ dē əm/ *n., pl.* **me•di•a** /mē′ dē ə/ *or* **me•di•ums.** a position between extremes. *The family reached a happy medium about what movie to see.*

mer•chan•dise¹ /mûr′ chən dīz′ *or* mûr′ chən dīs′/ *n.* goods for sale. *What kind of merchandise is for sale at that store?*

mer•chan•dise² /mûr′ chən dīz′/ *v.* **mer•chan•dised, mer•chan•dis•ing, mer•chan•dis•es.** to buy and sell goods. *These stores merchandise used clothing.* —**mer•chan•dis•er** *n.*

mer•chant /mûr′ chənt/ *n.* someone who owns a retail business. *The toy merchant moved to a larger store last year.*

me•ter¹ /mē′ tər/ *n.* a pattern of rhythm in lines of poetry. *Read the poem out loud so that you hear the meter.*

me•ter² /mē′ tər/ *n.* a unit of length in the metric system equal to 39.37 inches. *The piece of ribbon is one meter long.*

me•ter³ /mē′ tər/ *n.* a device used for measuring and recording time, distance, volume, or intensity. *The service person will check our meter to see how much gas we used last month.*

met•ric /mět′ rĭk/ *adj.* using a measurement system based on units of ten. *The recipe listed its ingredients in metric measurements.*

min•i•a•ture /mĭn′ ē ə chər *or* mĭn′ ə chər/ *adj.* on a greatly reduced size; little. *The miniature train is a model of a real steam engine.*

min•i•mize¹ /mĭn′ ə mīz′/ *v.* **min•i•mized, min•i•miz•ing, min•i•miz•es.** to make something smaller. *The manager tried to minimize the cost to the company.* —**min•i•mi•za•tion** *n.* —**min•i•miz•er** *n.*

min•i•mize² /mĭn′ ə mīz′/ *v.* **min•i•mized, min•i•miz•ing, min•i•miz•es.** to represent as having little importance or value. *Don't minimize the value of exercise.* —**min•i•mi•za•tion** *n.* —**min•i•miz•er** *n.*

min•i•mum¹ /mĭn′ ə məm/ *n., pl.* **min•i•mums** *or* **min•i•ma.** the least amount possible. *The game needs a minimum of four players.*

min•i•mum² /mĭn′ ə məm/ *adj.* representing the least amount possible. *The minimum wage has been raised.*

mi•nus¹ /mī′ nəs/ *prep.* decreased by subtraction. *Eight minus three equals five.*

mi•nus² /mī′ nəs/ *n., pl.* **min•us•es.** a dash that indicates subtraction. *Jay overlooked the minus and got the wrong answer.*

mi•nus³ /mī′ nəs/ *adj.* negative; less than zero. *The math problem ended with a minus value.*

mi•rage /mĭ räzh′/ *n.* something seen in the distance that is not really there. *The sailor thought he saw an island, but it was only a mirage.*

mis•rule¹ /mĭs rōōl′/ *v.* **mis•ruled, mis•rul•ing, mis•rules.** to rule poorly or unjustly. *A leader who misrules will soon lose support.*

mis•rule² /mĭs rōōl′/ *n.* poor leadership. *His misrule of the kingdom caused a revolt.*

mo•men•tar•i•ly /mō′ mən târ′ ə lē/ *adv.* very soon. *We will leave momentarily.*

mul•ti•ple¹ /mŭl′ tə pəl/ *adj.* more than one. *He received multiple injuries in the accident.*

PRONUNCIATION KEY	
/ă/	pat
/ā/	pay
/â/	care
/ä/	father
/är/	far
/ĕ/	pet
/ē/	be
/ĭ/	pit
/ī/	pie
/îr/	pier
/ŏ/	mop
/ō/	toe
/ô/	paw, for
/oi/	noise
/ou/	out
/ŏŏ/	look
/ōō/	boot
/ŭ/	cut
/ûr/	urge
/th/	thin
/th/	this
/hw/	what
/zh/	vision
/ə/	about
	item
	pencil
	gallop
	circus
/ər/	butter

mul•ti•ple² /mŭl′ tə pəl/ *n.* a number that can be divided evenly by another number. *The numbers 4 and 8 are multiples of 2.*

mys•te•ri•ous /mĭ stîr′ ē əs/ *adj.* unusual; different; cannot be understood. *The police investigated the mysterious disappearance of the car.* —**mys•te•ri•ous•ly** *adv.* —**mys•te•ri•ous•ness** *n.*

nar•rate /năr′ āt′ *or* nă rāt′/ *v.* **nar•rat•ed, nar•rat•ing, nar•rates.** to put into words; to tell in detail. *The teacher will narrate a story about two friends.*

nar•rat•or /năr′ rā′ tər/ *n.* a person who tells a story. *The narrator of the story is a young girl.*

nat•u•ral /năch′ ər əl *or* năch′ rəl/ *adj.* not artificial; produced by nature. *We have a natural lake in our town.* —**nat•u•ral•ly** *adv.* —**nat•u•ral•ness** *n.*

news /no͞oz *or* nyo͞oz/ *n.* information about a recent event. *We watched the news on TV.*

nov•el¹ /nŏv′ əl/ *adj.* new; different. *That is a novel way to decorate a birthday cake.* —**nov•el•ly** *adv.*

nov•el² /nŏv′ əl/ *n.* writing that tells a story. *I have read several good novels.*

nov•el•ty /nŏv′ əl tē/ *n., pl.* **nov•el•ties.** a new and unusual thing. *Carly's simple invention was a novelty.*

nu•mer•ous /no͞o′ mər əs *or* nyo͞o′ mər əs/ *adj.* many. *There are numerous choices on the dessert menu.* —**nu•mer•ous•ly** *adv.* —**nu•mer•ous•ness** *n.*

o•bey /ō bā′/ *v.* **o•beyed, o•bey•ing, o•beys.** to do what someone tells you. *You should obey the signal of the crossing guard when you cross the street.*

oc•cu•pa•tion¹ /ŏk′ yə pā′ shən/ *n.* a job. *Medicine is his occupation.*

oc•cu•pa•tion² /ŏk′ yə pā′ shən/ *n.* the act of holding or controlling a place. *Finally the region was free of foreign occupation.*

oc•cu•py¹ /ŏk′ yə pī′/ *v.* **oc•cu•pied, oc•cu•py•ing, oc•cu•pies.** to live in. *The new owners will occupy the house next spring.* —**oc•cu•pi•er** *n.*

oc•cu•py² /ŏk′ yə pī′/ *v.* **oc•cu•pied, oc•cu•py•ing, oc•cu•pies.** to take up or fill (time or space). *Homework occupied most of my weekend.* —**oc•cu•pi•er** *n.*

or•gan•ism /ôr′ gə nĭz′ əm/ *n.* a living thing. *There are many small organisms in a pond.*

or•gan•i•za•tion¹ /ôr′ gə nĭ zā′ shən/ *n.* a group of people with a purpose. *This organization helps children learn to read.* —**or•gan•i•za•tion•al** *adj.* —**or•gan•i•za•tion•al•ly** *adv.*

or•gan•i•za•tion² /ôr′ gə nĭ zā′ shən/ *n.* the condition of being orderly. *A neat desk is a sign of organization.* —**or•gan•i•za•tion•al** *adj.* —**or•gan•i•za•tion•al•ly** *adv.*

or•gan•iz•er /ôr′ gən īz′ ər/ *n.* one who puts something into order. *The organizer planned a fun party.*

par•a•graph /păr′ ə grăf′/ *n.* a group of sentences about a single idea. *I wrote a paragraph about my favorite book.*

per•cent /pər sĕnt′/ *n.* out of each hundred. *At least fifty percent of the people at the game wore red.*

pest¹ /pĕst/ *n.* an annoying person or thing. *My younger cousin can be a pest sometimes.*

pest² /pĕst/ *n.* a harmful plant or animal. *Mosquitoes are pests in the summer.*

plead /plēd/ *v.* **plead•ed** *or* **pled** /pled/, **plead•ing, pleads.** to appeal; to beg. *A lawyer will plead his case in court.* —**plead•a•ble** *adj.* —**plead•ing•ly** *adv.* —**plead•er** *n.*

plunge /plŭnj/ *v.* **plunged, plung•ing, plung•es.** to dive, fall, or move down suddenly. *The swimmer plunged into the cold water.*

po•em /pō′ əm/ *n.* creative writing that often uses comparisons, rhythm, and rhyme. *My brother wrote a funny poem about our vacation.*

pol•i•cy /pŏl′ ĭ sē/ *n., pl.* **pol•i•cies.** a plan of action. *Our group's policy is to admit new members in April.*

por•tray /pôr trā′ *or* pōr trā′/ *v.* **por•trayed, por•tray•ing, por•trays.** to show or tell about. *The writer portrayed Abraham Lincoln as very gentle.*

pre•cau•tion /prĭ kô′ shən/ *n.* an act to guard against an upcoming event. *Use precaution when approaching a strange dog.*

pred•a•tor /prĕd′ ə tər *or* prĕd′ ə tôr′/ *n.* an animal that relies on other animals for food. *There are many predators in nature.*

pre•dict /prĭ dĭkt′/ *v.* **pre•dict•ed, pre•dict•ing, pre•dicts.** to say what would happen in the future. *The farmer predicted when it would snow.* —**pre•dict•a•ble** *adj.* —**pre•dict•a•bly** *adv.*

pre•dic•tor /prĭ dĭk′ tər/ *n.* a thing or a person who tells what will happen in the future. *The gray clouds are a predictor of rain.*

prey¹ /prā/ *n.* an animal caught for food. *The prey for a coyote can be a rabbit.*

prey² /prā/ *v.* **preyed, prey•ing, preys.** to hunt for food. *Hawks prey on squirrels.*

print¹ /prĭnt/ *n.* a mark made upon a surface. *Our feet left prints in the sand.*

print² /prĭnt/ *v.* **print•ed, print•ing, prints.** to publish. *Our school prints a newsletter every week.*

pri•or¹ /prī′ ər/ *adj.* coming before; earlier. *I have a prior invitation, so I cannot come to your party.* —**pri•or•ly** *adv.*

pri•or² /prī′ ər/ *n.* the monk in charge of a monastery. *The prior welcomed visitors to the monastery.* —**pri•or•ate** *n.* —**pri•or•ship** *n.*

pro•duce¹ /prə dōōs′ *or* prə dyōōs′/ *v.* **pro•duced, pro•duc•ing, pro•duc•es.** to make or create. *We had to produce ten sentences using the new words.* —**pro•duc•i•ble** *adj.*

pro•duce² /prŏd′ ōōs *or* prō′ dōōs/ *n.* farm products. *The farmers brought their produce to market.*

pro•duct /prŏd′ əkt/ *n.* something made. *The new soap products sold quickly.*

pro•duc•tion /prə dŭk′ shən/ *n.* the process of making something. *The production of new games for computers has increased.*

pro•duc•tive /prə dŭk′ tĭv/ *adj.* having useful or good results. *We were very productive during our study time.* —**pro•duc•tive•ly** *adv.* —**pro•duc•tiv•i•ty** *n.* —**pro•duc•tive•ness** *n.*

pro•duc•tiv•i•ty /prō′ dŭk tĭv′ ĭ tē/ *n.* the quality of having useful or good results. *Our town admires the mayor's productivity.*

pro•nounce /prə nouns′/ *v.* **pro•nounced, pro•nounc•ing, pro•nounc•es.** to say a word in a certain way. *The teacher will pronounce the words for the spelling bee.* —**pro•nounce•a•ble** *adj.* —**pro•nounc•er** *n.*

pro•nun•ci•a•tion¹ /prə nŭn′ sē ā′ shən/ *n.* the way in which a word is spoken. *We practiced the pronunciation of each new word.*

pro•nun•ci•a•tion² /prə nŭn′ sē ā′ shən/ *n.* the phonetic writing of a word. *We wrote the phonetic pronunciation of the spelling words.*

punc•tu•al /pŭngk′ chōō əl/ *adj.* prompt; on time. *You must be punctual in arriving to school.* —**punc•tu•al•i•ty** *n.* —**punc•tu•al•ly** *adv.*

Q

qual•i•fi•ca•tion /kwŏl′ ə fĭ kā′ shən/ *n.* the condition of having needed requirements. *He has all of the qualifications for the job.*

qual•i•fy /kwŏl′ ə fī′/ *v.* **qual•i•fied, qual•i•fy•ing, qual•i•fies.** to do what is needed to meet requirements. *The runner qualified for the state track meet.*

R

reb•el¹ /rĕb′ əl/ *n.* a person who fights those in charge. *The rebel led a loud protest march.*

re•bel² /rĭ bĕl′/ *v.* **re•belled, re•bel•ling, re•bels.** to oppose authority. *The colonists rebelled when the king raised their taxes.*

PRONUNCIATION KEY	
/ă/	pat
/ā/	pay
/â/	care
/ä/	father
/är/	far
/ĕ/	pet
/ē/	be
/ĭ/	pit
/ī/	pie
/îr/	pier
/ŏ/	mop
/ō/	toe
/ô/	paw, for
/oi/	noise
/ou/	out
/ŏŏ/	look
/ōō/	boot
/ŭ/	cut
/ûr/	urge
/th/	thin
/th/	this
/hw/	what
/zh/	vision
/ə/	about
	item
	pencil
	gallop
	circus
/ər/	butter

re•bel•lion /rĭ bĕl′ yən/ *n.* an organized opposition of authority. *The Boston Tea Party was an act of rebellion against English rule.*

rec•og•nize /rĕk′ əg nīz′/ *v.* **rec•og•nized, rec•og•niz•ing, rec•og•niz•es.** to know or understand. *I recognize that boy from his picture.* —**rec•og•niz•a•ble** *adj.* —**rec•og•niz•a•bly** *adv.* —**rec•og•niz•er** *n.*

re•gal[1] /rē′ gəl/ *adj.* of or relating to a king or queen; royal. *The regal palace was beautiful.* —**re•gal•ly** *adv.*

re•gal[2] /rē′ gəl/ *adj.* suitable for a king or queen. *We received a regal welcome.* —**re•gal•ly** *adv.*

reg•u•la•tion /rĕg′ yə lā′ shən/ *n.* a rule; a law. *The hospital regulation allowed no visitors under the age of ten.*

reign[1] /rān/ *v.* **reigned, reign•ing, reigns.** to rule. *The queen reigned for many years.*

reign[2] /rān/ *n.* the time during which someone rules. *The reign of a king usually lasts until his death.*

re•in•force•ment[1] /rē′ ĭn fôrs′ mənt *or* rē′ ĭn fōrs′ mənt/ *n.* support. *Steel reinforcement made the building strong.*

re•in•force•ment[2] /rē′ ĭn fôrs′ mənt *or* rē′ ĭn fōrs′ mənt/ *n.* additional troops and supplies. *The much needed reinforcements encouraged the troops.*

re•lease[1] /rĭ lēs′/ *v.* **re•leased, re•leas•ing, re•leas•es.** to set free. *We released the bird from its cage.*

re•lease[2] /rĭ lēs′/ *n.* the act of setting free. *The release of the butterflies into the air was a pretty sight.*

re•new /rĭ nōō′ *or* rĭ nyōō′/ *v.* **re•newed, re•new•ing, re•news.** to restore; to start again. *My mother renewed the magazine subscription.* —**re•new•a•ble** *adj.* —**re•new•a•bly** *adv.* —**re•new•a•bil•i•ty** *n.*

ren•o•vate /rĕn′ ə vāt′/ *v.* **ren•o•vat•ed, ren•o•vat•ing, ren•o•vates.** to repair or to make like new. *The young couple renovated the old house.* —**re•no•va•tion** *n.* —**re•no•va•tor** *n.*

re•ply[1] /rĭ plī′/ *v.* **re•plied, re•ply•ing, re•plies.** to answer. *She will reply to my question.* —**re•pli•er** *n.*

re•ply[2] /rĭ plī′/ *n., pl.* **re•plies.** an oral or written answer. *I received a reply to my letter.* —**re•pli•er** *n.*

re•port[1] /rĭ pôrt′/ *v.* **re•port•ed, re•port•ing, re•ports.** to give information about something. *When the man saw the flames, he reported the fire.* —**re•port•a•ble** *adj.*

re•port[2] /rĭ pôrt′/ *n.* a detailed telling or writing about something. *Tom gave a report on his science project.* —**re•port•a•ble** *adj.*

re•port•er /rĭ pôr′ tər/ *n.* someone who writes or tells about the news. *The newspaper reporter wrote an article about recycling.*

re•quest[1] /rĭ kwĕst′/ *v.* **re•quest•ed, re•quest•ing, re•quests.** to ask for. *The invitation to the party requested a response.*

re•quest[2] /rĭ kwĕst′/ *n.* the act of asking. *We will make a request for two more tickets.*

re•spect[1] /rĭ spĕkt′/ *v.* **re•spect•ed, re•spect•ing, re•spects.** to show consideration for. *Members of a family should respect one another.*

re•spect[2] /rĭ spĕkt′/ *n.* a feeling of regard. *He had great respect for his grandmother.*

re•vise /rĭ vīz′/ *v.* **re•vised, re•vis•ing, re•vis•es.** to change. *The coaches are going to revise the hours of practice.* —**re•vis•a•ble** *adj.* —**re•vis•er** *n.* —**re•vis•or** *n.*

re•vive /rĭ vīv′/ *v.* **re•vived, re•viv•ing, re•vives.** to bring back to consciousness; to reawaken. *The doctor revived the woman who had been knocked unconscious in the accident.*

roam /rōm/ *v.* **roamed, roam•ing, roams.** to wander; to go from place to place without a plan. *The students roamed the school until the bell rang.*

route[1] /rōōt *or* rout/ *n.* the way from one place to another. *Which is the shortest route from my house to your house?*

route[2] /rōōt *or* rout/ *v.* **rout•ed, rout•ing, routes.** to send from one place to another. *Please route the envelope to the school office.*

rou•tine /rōō tēn′/ *n.* a fixed way of doing things. *The students follow a routine at lunchtime.* —**rou•tine•ly** *adv.*

roy•al /roi′ əl/ *adj.* splendid; fit for a king or queen. *The royal crown was covered with jewels.* —**roy•al•ly** *adv.*

rul•er¹ /rōō′ lər/ *n.* one who governs. *The rulers of the two countries met to talk about peace.*

rul•er² /rōō′ lər/ *n.* a straightedge for drawing and measuring. *Use your ruler to draw a square.*

— S —

scale¹ /skāl/ *v.* **scaled, scal•ing, scales.** to climb. *The group is preparing to scale the mountain.*

scale² /skāl/ *n.* the outer covering of fish, reptiles, and certain other animals. *The fish's scales gave it a shiny appearance.*

scale³ /skāl/ *n.* a machine for weighing. *The scale showed that I had three pounds of apples.*

sched•ule¹ /skĕj′ ōōl *or* skĕj′ ōō əl *or* skĕj′ əl/ *n.* a plan of upcoming events. *I asked for a bus schedule.*

sched•ule² /skĕj′ ōōl *or* skĕj′ ōō əl *or* skĕj′ əl/ *v.* **sched•uled, sched•ul•ing, sched•ules.** to plan for a certain time. *Our teacher schedules a special reading time for us every day.*

scope¹ /skōp/ *n.* everything that is involved. *That is not within the scope of my research.*

scope² /skōp/ *v.* **scoped, scop•ing, scopes.** to examine in detail. *She scoped the classroom for a place to sit.*

scrib•ble /skrĭb′ əl/ *v.* **scrib•bled, scrib•bling, scrib•bles.** to write in a hurried or careless way. *I scribbled a note to myself about the next assignment.* **—scrib•bler** *n.*

script /skrĭpt/ *n.* the written words of a play, broadcast, or movie. *The students wrote the script for tonight's performance.*

sense¹ /sĕns/ *v.* **sensed, sens•ing, sens•es.** to feel or understand. *I could sense that my friend did not understand the lesson.*

sense² /sĕns/ *n.* a function or power of awareness, especially hearing, seeing, smelling, touching, and tasting. *My sense of touch helped me find my way across the dark room.*

se•quel¹ /sē′ kwəl/ *n.* a literary work that continues an earlier story. *I am reading the sequel to the novel.*

se•quel² /sē′ kwəl/ *n.* something that follows; a result or consequence. *A poor grade is the sequel to not studying.*

se•ries /sîr′ ēz/ *n., pl.* **se•ries.** a number of books, movies, or programs that are grouped together. *The librarian suggested a series of books about airplanes.*

short•age /shôr′ tĭj/ *n.* not enough of something. *We had a shortage of crayons in art class.*

sig•nal¹ /sĭg′ nəl/ *n.* something that gives a message. *The driver stopped the car as the traffic signal turned red.*

sig•nal² /sĭg′ nəl/ *v.* **sig•naled, sig•nal•ing, sig•nals** *or* **sig•nalled, sig•nal•ling, sig•nals.** to make a sign. *We signal the bus driver when we want to get off the bus.* **—sig•nal•er** *or* **sig•nal•ler** *n.*

sig•na•ture /sĭg′ nə chər/ *n.* the writing of your own name. *Mary wrote her signature on the check.*

sig•nif•i•cant /sĭg nĭf′ ĭ kənt/ *adj.* important. *A significant change in the weather pattern caused snow.* **—sig•nif•i•cant•ly** *adv.*

sig•ni•fy /sĭg′ nə fī/ *v.* **sig•ni•fied, sig•ni•fy•ing, sig•ni•fies.** to mean something. *The white cane signified that the person was blind.* **—sig•ni•fi•er** *n.*

si•lence /sī′ ləns/ *n.* no sound. *There was complete silence in the theater.*

soar /sôr *or* sōr/ *v.* **soared, soar•ing, soars.** to fly or glide high. *The hawk soared above the trees.*

spec•tac•u•lar /spĕk tăk′ yə lər/ *adj.* sensational. *We took a spectacular picture of the mountains from our window.* **—spec•tac•u•lar•ly** *adv.*

spec•ta•tor /spĕk′ tā tər/ *n.* a person who watches or observes. *Jean was a spectator at the parade.*

speech•less /spēch′ lĭs/ *adj.* unable to speak. *We were speechless while the magician was on stage.* **—speech•less•ly** *adv.* **—speech•less•ness** *n.*

PRONUNCIATION KEY

/ă/	pat
/ā/	pay
/â/	care
/ä/	father
/är/	far
/ĕ/	pet
/ē/	be
/ĭ/	pit
/ī/	pie
/îr/	pier
/ŏ/	mop
/ō/	toe
/ô/	paw, for
/oi/	noise
/ou/	out
/ōō/	look
/ōō/	boot
/ŭ/	cut
/ûr/	urge
/th/	thin
/th/	this
/hw/	what
/zh/	vision
/ə/	about
	item
	pencil
	gallop
	circus
/ər/	butter

speed•om•e•ter /spĭ dŏm′ ĭ tər *or* spē dŏm′ ĭ tər/ *n.* an instrument that indicates speed. *Check your speedometer to see how fast you are going.*

stalk¹ /stôk/ *n.* the stem of a plant. *A sunflower stalk is very sturdy.*

stalk² /stôk/ *v.* **stalked, stalk•ing, stalks.** to move in a threatening way. *The cat stalked across our yard toward the bird feeder.* —**stalk•er** *n.*

stan•za /stăn′ zə/ *n.* a division of a poem. *I memorized the first stanza of the poem.*

state¹ /stāt/ *v.* **stat•ed, stat•ing, states.** to say. *The coach stated that the game was cancelled.*

state² /stāt/ *n.* one part of a country or nation. *Texas is a state in the United States.*

stat•ic /stăt′ ĭk/ *adj.* fixed; not changing. *The weather will not remain static.* —**stat•i•cal•ly** *adv.*

sta•tion•ar•y /stā′ shə nĕr′ ē/ *adj.* still; not moving. *We remained in a stationary position until the coach told us to move.*

stead•y¹ /stĕd′ ē/ *v.* **stead•ied, stead•y•ing, stead•ies.** to make steady or sure in movement. *Once we were through the rapids, we quickly steadied the raft.*

stead•y² /stĕd′ ē/ *adj.* **stead•i•er, stead•i•est.** constant; even. *We had a steady rain during the night.* —**stead•i•ly** *adv.* —**stead•i•ness** *n.*

stride¹ /strīd/ *v.* **strode** /strōd/ *or* **strid•den** /strĭd′ n/, **strid•ing, strides.** to walk with long steps, usually quickly. *The man strides across the yard to catch the bus.*

stride² /strīd/ *n.* progress or improvement. *Great strides are being made in the field of computer technology.*

strut /strŭt/ *v.* **strut•ted, strut•ting, struts.** to walk with self-importance. *The actor strutted across the stage.*

sub•scrip•tion /səb skrĭp′ shən/ *n.* a purchase for a specific time period, such as a magazine. *The subscription to the magazine was a gift.*

sum•ma•ry /sŭm′ ə rē/ *n., pl.* **sum•ma•ries.** a short statement that gives the main idea about something. *The reporter gave a summary of the events leading to the first moon landing.* —**sum•mar•i•ly** *adv.*

sup•ply¹ /sə plī′/ *v.* **sup•plied, sup•ply•ing, sup•plies.** to give things for people to use; to provide. *Does the school supply students with pencils and paper?* —**sup•pli•er** *n.*

sup•ply² /sə plī′/ *v.* **sup•plied, sup•ply•ing, sup•plies.** to make available (to satisfy a need or want). *The rains supplied relief from the hot, dry weather.* —**sup•pli•er** *n.*

sup•ply³ /sə plī′/ *n., pl.* **sup•plies.** the amount that is available. *Do we have a large supply of napkins for the party?*

sur•ren•der /sə rĕn′ dər/ *v.* **sur•ren•dered, sur•ren•der•ing, sur•ren•ders.** to give up. *The thief surrendered immediately.*

sur•vive /sər vīv′/ *v.* **sur•vived, sur•viv•ing, sur•vives.** to stay alive. *The baby bird survived its fall from the nest.* —**sur•vi•vor** *n.*

sus•pect¹ /sə spĕkt′/ *v.* **sus•pect•ed, sus•pect•ing, sus•pects.** to believe something you are not sure about. *I suspect that I will get a good grade on the spelling test.*

sus•pect² /sus′ pĕkt′/ *n.* a person who may have committed a crime. *The police arrested the suspect in the burglary.*

sus•pi•cious¹ /sə spĭsh′ əs/ *adj.* questionable; causing a lack of trust. *His suspicious actions made us all wonder what he was hiding.* —**sus•pi•cious•ly** *adv.* —**sus•pi•cious•ness** *n.*

sus•pi•cious² /sə spĭsh′ əs/ *adj.* untrusting. *We were suspicious of the dark clouds and thunder.* —**sus•pi•cious•ly** *adv.* —**sus•pi•cious•ness** *n.*

sym•bol /sĭm′ bəl/ *n.* a sign. *This bracelet will be a symbol of our friendship.*

T

tar•dy /tär′ dē/ *adj.* **tar•di•er, tar•di•est.** late. *The players should not be tardy to the basketball game.* —**tar•di•ly** *adv.* —**tar•di•ness** *n.*

te•di•ous /tē′ dē əs/ *adj.* slow; boring. *Washing the dinner dishes every night can be tedious.* —**te•di•ous•ly** *adv.* —**te•di•ous•ness** *n.*

tem•po•rar•y[1] /tĕm′ pə rĕr′ ē/ *adj.* lasting for a limited time. *High school students sometimes have temporary jobs in the summer.*

tem•po•rar•y[2] /tĕm′ pə rĕr′ ē/ *n., pl.* **tem•po•rar•ies.** an employee who works for a short time. *My brother is a temporary at the grocery store.*

term[1] /tûrm/ *n.* a limited period of time for something. *My sister taught for one term of the academic year.*

term[2] /tûrm/ *v.* **termed, term•ing, terms.** to call by a certain name. *He was termed a leader by his classmates.*

text /tĕkst/ *n.* the printed or written words. *This book has more pictures than text.*

time frame /tīm frām/ *n.* a period of time in which something is expected to happen. *The time frame for finishing our new house is six weeks.*

time•ly[1] /tīm′ lē/ *adj.* **time•li•er, time•li•est.** early; soon; quick. *I answered the invitation with a timely response.*

time•ly[2] /tīm′ lē/ *adj.* **time•li•er, time•li•est.** happening at the right time. *My boss left a timely message on my desk.*

ti•tle[1] /tīt′ l/ *n.* a name of a book, play, movie, song, or work of art. *The title of my favorite book is* Charlotte's Web.

ti•tle[2] /tīt′ l/ *n.* a legal claim to ownership. *We keep the title to our house in a safe place.*

ti•tle[3] /tīt′ l/ *n.* a word that shows a person's rank, occupation, or status. *The student felt proud to earn the title "Doctor."*

to•tal[1] /tōt′ l/ *n.* the sum; the whole quantity. *Give me the total when you figure it out.*

to•tal[2] /tōt′ l/ *adj.* complete. *We were in total darkness.* —**to•tal•ly** *adv.*

to•tal[3] /tōt′ l/ *v.* **to•taled, to•tal•ing, to•tals** *or* **to•talled, to•tal•ling, to•tals.** to add up; to find the sum. *Total the column of numbers.*

trace[1] /trās/ *n.* a sign that something has been in that place. *After she cleaned her room, there was not a trace of dirt.*

trace[2] /trās/ *v.* **traced, trac•ing, trac•es.** to follow the path of. *We traced the cookie crumbs to Benjamin.* —**trace•a•ble** *adj.* —**trace•a•bly** *adv.*

trace[3] /trās/ *v.* **traced, trac•ing, trac•es.** to copy. *The children will trace their names with different colors of paint.* —**trace•a•ble** *adj.* —**trace•a•bly** *adv.*

trans•la•tion /trăns lā′ shən *or* trănz lā′ shən/ *n.* a written or spoken expression of something in a different language. *This is an English translation from a French story.*

tri•al[1] /trī′ əl *or* trīl/ *n.* a test of one's patience or ability. *My little sister can be a trial at times.*

tri•al[2] /trī′ əl *or* trīl/ *n.* the hearing of a case in court. *His case comes to trial next week.*

un•fore•seen /ŭn′ fər sēn′ *or* ŭn′ fôr sēn′/ *adj.* unexpected; without warning. *We were surprised by the unforeseen storm.*

un•just /ŭn jŭst′/ *adj.* unfair. *The people revolted against the tyrant's unjust rules.* —**un•just•ly** *adv.* —**un•just•ness** *n.*

urge /ûrj/ *v.* **urged, urg•ing, urg•es.** to try strongly to convince. *The teachers urge us to read over the summer.*

verse /vûrs/ *n.* a line or lines in a poem or song. *Each student read a verse of the poem for the audience.*

vic•to•ri•ous /vĭk tôr′ ē əs *or* vĭk tōr′ ē əs/ *adj.* being the winner. *The victorious soccer team had a party to celebrate.* —**vic•to•ri•ous•ly** *adv.* —**vic•to•ri•ous•ness** *n.*

view[1] /vyōō/ *v.* **viewed, view•ing, views.** to look at with the eyes. *We viewed a movie about guide dogs.*

view[2] /vyōō/ *n.* the act of looking at something. *Our first view of the ocean was very exciting.*

PRONUNCIATION KEY	
/ă/	pat
/ā/	pay
/â/	care
/ä/	father
/är/	far
/ĕ/	pet
/ē/	be
/ĭ/	pit
/ī/	pie
/îr/	pier
/ŏ/	mop
/ō/	toe
/ô/	paw, for
/oi/	noise
/ou/	out
/ŏŏ/	look
/ōō/	boot
/ŭ/	cut
/ûr/	urge
/th/	thin
/th/	this
/hw/	what
/zh/	vision
/ə/	about
	item
	pencil
	gallop
	circus
/ər/	butter

view³ /vyo͞o/ *n.* a scene. *We had a nice view of the lake as we drove down the road.*

vi•o•late /vī′ ə lāt′/ *v.* **vi•o•lat•ed, vi•o•lat•ing, vi•o•lates.** to break a law, rule, or promise. *We did not mean to violate any rules.* —**vi•o•la•tor** *n.*

vis•i•ble /vĭz′ ə bəl/ *adj.* can be seen with the eye. *The house was not visible from the street.* —**vis•i•bly** *adv.* —**vis•i•ble•ness** *n.*

vis•it¹ /vĭz′ ĭt/ *v.* **vis•it•ed, vis•it•ing, vis•its.** to spend time in a place. *My family will visit my aunt in Florida this summer.*

vis•it² /vĭz′ ĭt/ *n.* a short time spent in a certain place. *I had a nice visit at my friend's house after school.*

vi•tal¹ /vīt′ l/ *adj.* necessary for life. *Oxygen is vital for most living things.* —**vi•tal•ly** *adv.*

vi•tal² /vīt′ l/ *adj.* very important. *Plenty of sleep is vital to good health.* —**vi•tal•ly** *adv.*

vi•ta•min /vī′ tə mĭn/ *n.* things in food needed for human growth and health. *Some vegetables have lots of vitamins.*

vo•cab•u•lar•y /vō kăb′ yə lĕr′ ē/ *n., pl.* **vo•cab•u•lar•ies.** all the words used by a person or group of people. *I have added many new words to my vocabulary this year.*

vo•cal /vō′ kəl/ *adj.* made or performed by the voice. *The choir's vocal performance was moving.* —**vo•cal•ly** *adv.*

vo•cal•ist /vō′ kə lĭst/ *n.* a singer. *The vocalist had a very high voice.*

vow•el¹ /vou′ əl/ *n.* the speech sounds made by the letters *a, e, i, o,* and *u.* *You say a vowel with your mouth open.*

vow•el² /vou′ əl/ *n.* any of the letters *a, e, i, o, u,* and sometimes *y. Write the vowels on the chalkboard.*

wealth•y /wĕl′ thē/ *adj.* **wealth•i•er, wealth•i•est.** rich. *My cousin's family is wealthy.* —**wealth•i•ly** *adv.* —**wealth•i•ness** *n.*

wilt /wĭlt/ *v.* **wilt•ed, wilt•ing, wilts.** to droop. *Flowers will wilt if they are not watered.*

Ⓩ

zo•ol•o•gist /zō ŏl′ ə jĭst/ *n.* a scientist who studies animals. *The zoologist came to our class to talk about wolves.*

Editorial Development: Cottage Communications

Design and Production: Bill SMITH STUDIO

Cover Illustration: Dave Cutler

Photo and Illustration Credits: Page 6, Whitman, Chelsea, Mass./Library of Congress; 28, PhotoDisc; 50, Photos.com; 72, PhotoDisc; 94, 116, Clipart.com; 138, Marc Brown Studios; 160, Clipart.com; 182, Bettmann/Corbis

Borders and Icons: Brock Waldron

Context Clues Strategies: Adapted from Camille Blachowicz and Peter J. Fisher. *Teaching Vocabulary in All Classrooms.* (2002). New Jersey: Merrill/Prentice Hall. p. 26

Printed in the United States of America   07 08 09 10 330 8 7 6 5 4